LISTENING TO ETERNITY

Photo: Mats Lundqvist

Tommie Haglund, 2018.

Praise for *Listening to Eternity*

Haglund's music—and his personal story—is a spiritual revelation in an otherwise spirit-poor time. Such a book is an important contribution to the literature on Swedish classical music and is written in such a way that it is accessible to the wide audience that has taken his music to their heart.

Erik Wallrup, Associate Professor of Aesthetics at Södertörn University, Stockholm, and author of *Being Musically Attuned: The Act of Listening to Music.*

Listening to Eternity is a timely book. Gracefully written, poised and insightful, it offers an intimate and engaging portrait of one of Sweden's hidden secrets. Tommie Haglund is that rare example of a composer who has heard the heavenly choirs and has devoted his life to sharing the experience.

Stephen McNeilly, Swedenborg Society Executive Director

Tommie Haglund is a composer for whom everything is connected. There is not a meaningless note in his work, no padding, no superficial effects, only a presence so deep that it intervenes in the serious listener's life. How everything is charged with meaning becomes even clearer when you read his biography.

Torbjörn Elensky, Author, Culture Writer and Essayist

A powerful and beautiful book! I was engrossed in every detail. Yardumian takes us on a fascinating journey as he opens our ears, minds and hearts to the transformational music of the highly lauded

Swedish composer Tommie Haglund, connecting us to our "inner universe", our "sanctuary for the soul". This is an inspirational story of human suffering . . . and the joy of transcendence, through the harmonicity of Artistic Musical Creativity, personal resilience, incandescence, empathy, subtlety and authenticity, guided by Truth.

Chika Robertson, Professor of Violin, The Royal Academy of Music, London

In this beautiful array of scintillating and sometimes shockingly personal interviews, readers are given a rare glimpse into the inner life of one of Scandinavia's greatest contemporary classical composers. Not just lovers of classical music will find much of interest in this kaleidoscopic take on Tommie Haglund's life and work—anyone who has sensed a mystical glimmer of wonder and awe behind the everyday, or become attuned to their own patterns of synchronicities (or, in Swedenborgian terms, correspondences) can resonate with the arc of Haglund's story, a journey that spans from coastal Sweden to rural France, Maggie Thatcher's drab England of the 1980's to smoke-filled secret initiation rituals of the Ojibwa in Canada. Haglund's music remains little known outside of Europe, and this book broadens an appreciation for not only his essential place in the broader development of modern classical music, but also that special category of visionary Swedish artists—among them August Strindberg and Hilma af Klint—whose work bears the imprint of their intense encounters with the works of Swedenborg.

Devin Zuber, Associate Professor of American Studies, Religion, & Literature, Graduate Theological Union, Berkeley

LISTENING TO ETERNITY

THE MUSIC, SPIRITUALITY, AND CREATIVE WORLD OF COMPOSER TOMMIE HAGLUND

Aram Yardumian

SWEDENBORG FOUNDATION
Royersford, Pennsylvania

LIBRARY OF CONGRESS CATALOGING-IN-PUBLICATION DATA

Yardumian, Aram.

Listening to eternity : the music, spirituality, and creative world of composer Tommie Haglund / by Aram Yardumian.

Royersford, PA : Swedenborg Foundation, 2025.

Includes bibliographical references.

LCCN 2024053861 | ISBN 9780877853664 (paperback)

ISBN 9780877857365 (ebook)

LCSH: 1. Haglund, Tommie, 1959– 2. Composers—Sweden—Biography. 3. Music—Sweden—History and criticism. 4. Spirituality in music.

LCGFT: Biographies.

LCC ML410.H1028365 Y37 2025

DDC 780.92 [B]--dc23/eng/20241115

LC record available at https://lccn.loc.gov/2024053861

Typesetting by Karen Connor

Cover design by Karen Connor

All images used with permission.

Swedenborg Foundation

70 Buckwalter Road

Suite 900 PMB 405

Royersford, PA 19468

www.swedenborg.com

Understand that you are another world
in miniature and that there is within you
the sun, the moon, and the stars.

—Origen, *Liviticum Homiliae*

Throughout the whole night I felt as if I were going down deep, stairs after stairs, and passing through various rooms; yet I was confident and felt safe, as if there were no danger in the depth.

—Emanuel Swedenborg, *Journal of Dreams*

For never
He could find words enough
To say about kindness, then, and to soothe, when
He saw it, the wrath of the world

—Friedrich Hölderlin, *Patmos*

Contents

Acknowledgments

Beyond the many people, too numerous to mention, who have had an impact on the life and works of Tommie Haglund, the following are those without whom this book would have been impossible:

Elisabet Löfberg Haglund, Victoria Haglund, Ingmar Simonsson, Anna-Lena Löfberg, Erik Wallrup, Charlotte Herrlin Johnsson, Anders Hallengren, Osman Alpsoy, Tony Lundman, Rachel Longstaff, Devin Zuber, Marvin Clymer and Carroll Odhner at Swedenborgiana, Sven-Erik Dymne, and Ulf Fembro. Great thanks also to the Interlibrary Loan and Circulation staff at the University of Pennsylvania's Van Pelt Library.

Author's Preface

THIS BOOK CHRONICLES the extended conversation I held with Swedish composer Tommie Haglund between 2014 and 2021. A Swedish language edition of this book was published in 2022 by Themis förlag in cooperation with the Swedenborg Society. I am grateful to now see an English edition published by the Swedenborg Foundation.

Haglund was born on January 15, 1959, in Kalmar, a town in which his family is deeply rooted and a town with, in turn, deep pre-Swedish roots in the Stone Age of Scandinavia. The story of Haglund's life and musical career is not that of Mozart, that is to say, not one of cultured prodigiousness and almost overbearing family support in childhood, nor does it resemble the life of Bo Nilsson, who leaped untrained into the upper echelons of musical prophecy. Haglund's story isn't typical in any way within the canon of classical composers, not simply because he seems to stand outside it, his influences all but buried alive in the compositions, or because a serious composer must live and work a certain way, but rather because as an artist he listens only to his own inner voice, to deeply personal demands, which, for better or worse, can never be met. And these inner demands, which so often run contrary to those of everyday life, to audience expectations and critical reception, so often fade away in the halls of the conservatory. Haglund is well-known in Sweden, where his compositions are performed regularly and where he receives the highest sort of national awards, but this reputation has taken a long time to build. His compositions have also been performed in the USA, Canada, the UK, France, Germany, Hungary, Austria, Bulgaria, Morocco, and Colombia, as well as in the Scandinavian countries. This book traces the circumstances of his life, from early childhood visions through his chance encounter with the works of Swedenborg[1] and the strange days of physical impairment to the present. Through the events, we see the unfolding of a parallel inner world and the need to see this world and express it musically. Haglund's creative methods are anything but textbook, and the voice in which he answers my questions is not tuned for broadcast media. If, at times, it seems I am reaching for extraneous detail, this is because, in Haglund's biographic details, there is more than enough turmoil and blessing for several lifetimes.

The images we chose for this book are deliberately low-fidelity, high-contrast snapshots that we thought captured the bleed and haze of memories better than professional commissions. They are a form of evidence that sometimes support and sometimes crash into the text. The conversations themselves were held mostly between 2015 and 2018, with a few additional words from the three years thereafter. We

---

1 Emanuel Swedenborg (1688–1772) was a Swedish scientist, theologian, and mystic, whose ideas inspired Swedenborgianism.

conversed at the composer's home in Halmstad and while walking in the nearby streets and forests. In fact, our dialogue began a few years earlier, when he and his wife Elisabet visited the USA, and we met to follow up on a review I wrote of his *Hymnen an die Nacht* CD. Halfway through the night, I suggested we start recording all the remarkable things he was telling me.

But really, this project began earlier than that. While listening to *Hymnen an die Nacht*, I was reading a book called *The Generous Earth* by Philip Oyler. It felt like a passage from the final track, "To the Sunset Breeze," settles into a pastoral vista that fits inside Oyler's depiction of the Dordogne Valley, France, in which the land doubles as an *entendre* for life itself, and so precisely that it seemed as if Haglund was channeling the experience, or somehow directly was aware of it. When I told him about this in an email, he replied, bewildered, that no, he was not thinking about that book while composing, but what a peculiar synchronicity since Philip Oyler had been acquainted with Delius (1862-1934)[2]—whose importance to Haglund in his early years cannot be overstated—and further, that Oyler's daughter, Soldanella, had been one of the most important people in his life. Soldanella is significant all the more so because she is the one who introduced Haglund to Swedenborg.

ARAM YARDUMIAN,
Berlin, Germany

---

2 Frederick Delius (1862–1934) was an English composer who lived abroad, in France, Germany, and the United States, for much of his professional life.

Introduction

A PRELUDE

ONE WONDERS AT times quite what the ordinary member of the public imagines a composer to be . . . in the past, a somewhat aloof, aristocratic figure, as perhaps portrayed on the silver screen, in a silk dressing gown, an expensive cigarette in a long holder, a brandy to the side, sat at a grand piano carefully considering, through the smoke, a minor detail in the score; or alternatively perhaps a tormented, disheveled individual, hunched before a battered upright piano, hair all over the place, maybe rough and uncouth in appearance, empty wine and beer bottles scattered around a dingy, top-floor garret, frantically attempting to retrieve the passionate ideas that have been churning around in their mind.

Of course, Tommie Haglund, who I am happy to claim as a close and dear friend, is neither of these; he sensibly does not smoke, though he will partake of a carefully selected glass of claret to accompany one of his frequent fabulous dinners, which are often of pure invention as if clutched from the ether! The reader will find a scholarly and authoritative "postlude" by Aram Yardumian (Epilogue) celebrating Tommie's artistic gifts elsewhere in this volume, but suffice it to say that he is straightforward, gentle, quiet, almost self-effacing, and without a negative bone in his body; he maintains an almost boyish demeanor which he has had since our first meeting back in the very early 1980s.

I sometimes think about how difficult it must be for a composer to create a sound world that is very much one's own. Performers have to take, at times, harsh criticism; this is the way of the world. But for a composer, devoting weeks, or more likely months, to creating a huge orchestral work, for example, must, at times, seem like walking on eggshells. Therefore, the huge success achieved by Tommie Haglund is to be admired, for he has shown he can produce the most musically deep and complex pieces that can, at the same time, touch the soul of the ordinary person in the street.

Many have been the times when visiting the Haglund household, I was greeted by the composer sitting at the piano, the floor strewn with seemingly dozens of sheets of manuscript paper, in no set order and containing the most complex penciled sketches of musical notation. "Come in, sit down over there. Now, what do you think of this opening?" And immediately, these magical sounds almost from another world envelope one. "Not too bad, is it?" comes the jaunty afterthought. "No, Tommie, it's great!"

Of course, our earliest times together were when Tommie was studying classical guitar with me in England, as well as the private sessions. He also attended several of our four- to five-day courses set in the beautiful house and gardens of Burton Manor College, a few miles north of Chester. This was a very special time with a wonderfully positive atmosphere of guitar playing, combined with the sheer joy of making music and a great feeling of comradeship in the classes. What also emerged then, and rather unexpectedly, was Tommie's infectious sense of humor. We often had evening student concerts in the impressive library, and at one of these was a small ensemble performing their prepared item. All had gone fairly well, if at a cautious tempo, until, for some reason, the piece began to disintegrate, with unrest and titters welling up from the audience. Tommie, who was a page-turner in this performance, was trying to control himself, shoulders heaving, his teeth firmly embedded in his thumb! The strangulated performance, gradually descending into chaos, finally ground to a halt a few bars before the end, the room filling with uncontrolled laughter and Tommie finding it hard to hold himself together. However, one dignified member of the audience, a well-known British historian and author who was there with his wife, was observed storming out, making it clear in no uncertain terms that the whole thing was a total disgrace! A footnote to this might be that, at this time, Tommie had not really considered composition as a full-time profession. Luckily, this incident did not put him off!

Another occasion was a visit to the cinema for the Monty Python film *The Life of Brian* shortly after its general release. By the final minutes, Tommie was so convulsed with laughter, which he was desperately trying to suppress, that he ended up in the aisle on his hands and knees. Somebody in the row behind even asked if he was having a seizure or cardiac arrest and if they should inform the staff.

Even these days, there is this juxtaposing of the intensely serious elements in Tommie's life with the complete opposite, a need for humor and, if you like, release. Many times, when relaxing after dinner, on come films like Laurel and Hardy or *Fawlty Towers* (John Cleese is a big fan of Tommie's music). This is not unusual. For example, a fine cellist I have worked with over the years does the same. In his case, he is an avid fan of Buster Keaton.

There is the term "seminal moment," and I have a sense that Tommie has experienced a number of these in his life. An important event happened one evening at the flat he was renting in Surbiton after we had had dinner. I had "discovered" the Violin Concerto by Frederick Delius some twenty years before this. It was a work I found intensely emotional and stopped me in my tracks, so I was keen to see what Tommie thought of it. Being on a cassette and forgetful on my part, we first had to go out to buy batteries for the player!

Now, Delius is one of those composers one either loves or detests. For me, his idyllic music was as if opening a door to a secret world. The violin concerto, though written in France, is for me imbued with a strong English character—depicting, perhaps, a warm summer afternoon, the special light subtly shifting and changing moment by moment, a brief rain shower, then drifting to a calm and glorious evening, in all the vibrant colors of nature, stretching out as though one doesn't want it to end and with a bittersweet feeling of nostalgia and deep longing—a day that will never return. One could tell Tommie was intensely moved by this music, and as you will read in this fascinating book, much of Tommie Haglund's life has revolved around the music of Delius, as well as other Impressionist and post-Impressionist composers.

The man who became Delius' amanuensis, Eric Fenby, was somebody Tommie would eventually meet. At one of those meetings, Tommie showed Fenby some of his music. I was away, but my parents said Tommie was in a terrible, but understandable, state of nerves that day before taking the train to Waterloo in London. Eric has now become a good friend and offered considerable support and encouragement to Tommie in his compositional career.

With Tommie Haglund, this famous humor was to appear again when we took our son Richard, still only in his teens, to meet Tommie for the first time at his gracious home in Halmstad. Entering the music room, he was somewhat shocked to see the composer slumped in something like a bath chair, swathed in blankets, wearing dark glasses, and hands drooping with the appearance of a very, very ill person! The disguise came off moments later with great hilarity, but of course, Tommie was copying how Delius looked in his last years when Eric Fenby first arrived at the Delius house in France in the 1920s, the scene depicted in the Ken Russell film *Song of Summer*.

What Tommie Haglund has done over the decades is create his own very special and, indeed, personal style of compositional technique and musical language. There is also, however, an almost inevitable search for nostalgia that was so prevalent with some of the early mid-twentieth-century composers; this is reflected in his use of orchestral color and orchestration. As a guitarist, Tommie played from quite an early age, but I was humbled and moved to learn that later he was greatly taken by my musical style and tone color. He also developed a great respect for the playing of British guitarist Julian Bream, whose inspired work had flowed logically and naturally into the world of the Renaissance lute, with superb recordings and recitals featuring composers such as John Dowland, Robert Johnson, Francis Cutting, and many more. This wonderful music resonated with Tommie, making a large impact, I believe, even before I met him, and it has become an intrinsic part of his musical makeup. I sense his first meeting with Bream was another of those seminal moments.

Over the past few years, the Tommie Haglund Festival has taken place every two years in Halmstad. This important event brings together many celebrated artists and ensembles, one of the more recent collaborations being with the Bogotá Philharmonic Orchestra, who are now a major force in the performance of Tommie's music. At the same time, Tommie is increasingly in demand for lectures and seminars at important musical centers of learning in Sweden and abroad. In support of so much work, Tommie is fortunate to have his wife, Elisabet, and four daughters, Amanda, Victoria (Vicky), Julia, and Clara. Whenever there is a family gathering, the house is full of female laughter, with doting paternal adoration in equal measures. It is this ongoing loving and stable family environment that continues to sustain and support the composer, the calmness and space enabling him to further his lifelong passion and mission.

I was delighted and surprised when Tommie said he was working on a piece entitled "To the Sunset Breeze" for harp, guitar, and string quartet to celebrate my fiftieth birthday. In it were references to Frederick Delius, and we gave the first performance at the Wigmore Hall, London in September 1997. Here, the guitar assumes more the role of a chamber instrument, not the main solo line as is found in most works of this type, with the guitar, as it were, successfully and skillfully weaving its way in and out of the other players.

Referring earlier to the scattered pages of manuscript usually surrounding Tommie's piano, one day, several such pages were thrust into my hand by the composer. He explained it was an earlier work for guitar, which, for some reason, had been put aside. What did I make of it, and could the ideas be drawn together to make a concert work? My first faltering steps at attempting to sight read this piece must not have encouraged Tommie, for it was a highly complex score. However, after taking it away for some time, and with a few minor revisions from the composer, including a new ending, it eventually became a fine, substantial concert work entitled "Beyond Farewell."

With the ever-growing catalog of Tommie Haglund works—the concertos, the searingly beautiful pieces for voice and orchestra, chamber works, etc.—logically, there had to come a time when he felt moved to compose a symphony, and what a work it turned out to be! An overwhelming sensory wash of sound in massive contrasting waves of emotion—a magnum opus if ever there was one. In a way, perhaps, this monumental piece reflects the somewhat turbulent history of his life, with terrible bouts of illness set against deeply emotionally fulfilling periods. All of this unfolds in the pages ahead. And just as one must open a book, so too must the listener "open the door" and let the emotions Tommie Haglund offers flood the imagination. We are all a part of Nature, and we must embrace this beauty and open one's mind and eyes to those beautiful moments, not just the bright afternoons and vivid, glowing orange-red sundowns, but also *taking time* away from the harsh glare of city lights to look at the wonders of the night sky, where it can feel as though one is falling into the seemingly endless firmament. These are things we will find in the music of Tommie Haglund—they are a gift from the composer—we just have to open that door.

JOHN MILLS,
Classical Guitarist
June 2024
Wiltshire, England

LISTENING
TO
ETERNITY

Part One

IRRESISTIBLE SOUND

Photo: Margreth Karlsson

Haglund Family, ca. 1970

1: EARLY YEARS

ARAM: How did it all begin? Did you grow up in a musical household?

TOMMIE: You know, I met my aunt Margreth—my father's sister—a couple of years ago. My parents hired her as a nanny during my first two years. She was sixteen when I was born. My first musical memory is her voice. She wasn't otherwise very musical—I'm not even sure whether she even sang in tune, but there was something in the sound of her voice. She and my grandmother used to make up their own songs and lyrics and sing them to me. It wasn't a soprano. It was sort of a long, soft alto voice. Anyway, I met her recently. She's deeply religious now; the rest of the family is not. When I met her she told me I wouldn't have survived into adulthood if I hadn't had the music. She probably meant mentally, but perhaps physically as well.

ARAM: What did the family listen to?

TOMMIE: Most of the music I grew up with was commercial music—music for entertainment. But no matter what genre, music

Photo: Unknown

Tommie Haglund, ca. 1965

has, as long as I can remember, offered me protection, a world of its own where no one could reach or harm me, and that is still true today. My mother told me many times that even before I was one year of age, I was absorbed by the gramophone. When I was two, I knew exactly which songs were on the records by looking at the labels. If we were guests somewhere, I would be immediately in front of the record player and would want to listen to music. And she still remembers how difficult it was to stop me once I had started listening.

ARAM: Do you still hear your aunt Margreth's voice when you compose now, or was its importance only in historical memory?

Photo: Tage Haglund

Tommie Haglund as a child with his aunt Margreth, early 1960s.

TOMMIE: I sometimes try to recapture her voice. The heart of my music started with that voice. She and both my grandparents were important to my sense of security. There are certain sounds in the opening to the *Miraggio* where I try to return to that memory of being consoled by a song. Not the high-pitched soprano voice in the piece but the emotional atmosphere of it. I told Margreth when I met her that I remember her voice still and how much it meant to me.

ARAM: You have two siblings?

TOMMIE: Yes, I have a younger sister, Jeanette, and a brother, Håkan.

ARAM: You did not have the best of relationships with your father. It may sound strange to ask but did this in any way inspire you to create?

TOMMIE: It's difficult to talk about that. I think one of the reasons why my anxiety is so easily aroused is that relationship. It wasn't a good relationship. We didn't understand each other. You couldn't argue with him, and if you didn't obey, the consequences could be out of proportion. Still, today, I can get angry and upset thinking about it. But I definitely don't want to be too hard on him because it's difficult to know what goes on inside another human being. But we were never close. He could be moved by all sorts of music, and he liked the energy and rhythm of certain things. I remember that he enjoyed listening to Sinatra and Ella Fitzgerald, as well as Beethoven's Fifth Symphony, and once he told me he liked Stravinsky's *Rite of Spring*. Later in life, I felt he was sincerely proud of what I accomplished as a composer and emphasized that I did it with hardly any support from home. He died this summer, and before the end, he apologized for having hit me so much. In my heart, I reconciled with him. But it still affects me. It was easier to communicate with my mother.

You know, when I was young, I spent one and a half years in the hospital. I had this severe pain in my stomach because I lived under such stress as a child, particularly my father's anger. They put me in the hospital, and they discovered an abnormal growth in my small intestine.

ARAM: An ulcer, maybe?

TOMMIE: No, some other kind of growth. It was very serious. I was sent down to Lund for examinations. One and a half years

I spent in a hospital in Kalmar—from age seven to eight-and-a-half. I was alone often, and the examinations were very painful. I understood there was a potential risk. I thought, perhaps I won't make it. I'll probably end up somewhere in heaven. So, I wanted to read about the universe. I borrowed lots of books about space, the planets, and nebulae—piles of books. In the hospital, you have a bed, a little side table, and a radio with FM and AM. You had an earphone so you could listen. When you turned on AM in those days, you got Radio Luxembourg, German radio, and all that. But what caught my attention was the space between the stations; there was a noise. *Shhhhhhkkkkhhhh.* I pretended I was traveling in space, guided by the noise. I visualized how it all would look, guided by the sound.

ARAM: Did you continue to do that for one and a half years?

TOMMIE: I listened to it a lot, and I really looked forward every day to being alone, having the whole night free with no food, no nurses coming in, or whatever.

ARAM: It must have been strange to return to school after one and a half years.

TOMMIE: I recovered, but I was quite frail. I couldn't go to school or do athletics. I was too weak, so during football games, I mainly stood on the sidelines and pretended I was commentating for television. [*Laughs.*]

ARAM: It sounds like the radio was very important to you.

TOMMIE: Yes, one day, I went in the car with my grandfather. It was in the autumn. I was nine years old, and we were going to the summerhouse. The radio was on, and my grandfather said with a determined voice, "Listen to this. This is important." There was

Photo: Elsa Haglund

Tommie Haglund with his mother and sister, Kalmar Castle, ca. early 1960s.

some quiz on the radio. The question was, "What film is this music from?" It was Mozart's Piano Concerto No. 21 from *Elvira Madigan*. I had hardly heard any classical music, and I was enchanted. It was light and dark at the same time.

ARAM: What else did you hear at a young age that made an impression?

TOMMIE: Well, Owe Thörnquist, for example. Mainly sort of pop music, nothing really. Benny Andersson from ABBA had a group called Hep Stars. We listened to that. But when I heard Mozart, I discovered there was an atmosphere in it that resembled—sounds stupid—but it resembled the atmosphere of lying in hospital listening to radio noise. But now the sounds were organized.

ARAM: So, you were actually listening to radio static before classical music.

TOMMIE: Yes. There was something magical in that sound, far beyond the monotony of the hospital. When I listened to Mozart with my grandfather that day in the car, I thought this was a state I wanted to create. But how could I even approach such a wavelength when I knew nothing about the fundamentals of music? That's when I decided I wanted to compose. It was a crucial moment—when things really started.

Another important event at that time was my dad taking me to hear Lennart Annemark, who was an organist at the Kalmar Cathedral. He was mentioned in Sohlman's dictionary of musical names. He was quite famous. I remember him as a very kind man. He conducted the cathedral's boys' choir. I applied to the choir and was accepted. I understood later it was important for my development, and it must have been where I learned to read music. I remember when we were singing from the choir loft during the sermon, and he played solo works by Bach. It was magnificent.

ARAM: But you didn't just start composing on your own.

TOMMIE: No, because I didn't know how. Later, I had guitar lessons at school with this really boring old man. He should have been sitting in a bank office. He made me play these basic phrases, so I got fed up with it after a term and quit. A few months later, a different teacher phoned me and asked me to come around. I said no, but he convinced me to come to the next lesson to see what it was like. So, I went and met him. That was my first meeting with Claes-Göran Bjerding—what a character. I remember him stepping out of a white Mercedes Benz, wearing gabardine pants with bell bottoms, a large mustache and sideburns, and a necklace with a peace sign. He played trumpet in a *dansband*—you know, sort of a mix of schlager and country-western music. The band was named Claes-Freddys med Eva. He was a self-taught, all-round musician who specialized in trumpet and also did big band jazz arrangements and stuff like that. At the second lesson, I went right up to him and said, "I want to write music like Mozart."

"Oh," he said. "Fine, fine, I'll help you." That was his attitude.

ARAM: He was very important to you.

TOMMIE: Yes, and extremely gifted. One of the best teachers I've ever had, in one sense. His persistence is still with me. But he wasn't into classical music. His aim was primarily to give people the music they wanted, and that did not exclude classical music, but mainly, he was into so-called entertainment music. When I composed something, he always made sure it was performed. He was also the one who played the Baroque trumpet on this small piece I composed when I was eleven and another piece I wrote for oboe, harpsichord, and strings. When I was fourteen, I was asked by my confirmation priest, Gustaf Lagerquist, to write something for the service when he was to be appointed vicar by the bishop in Ljungbyholm. It was a piece for violin, flute, organ, and guitar—Claes-Göran supervised it. Then, when I was fifteen, he suggested I write my own arrangement of the final movement of Beethoven's Ninth to be performed by the school choir and orchestra as if it were the simplest thing in the world. He planned for me to also conduct it in the Ljungbyholm church for the school commencement. We all gathered in this church at the end of each term to sing hymns. That's what Sweden was like in those days.

ARAM: Do you think Claes-Göran has come to be more important in retrospect, or was he in your thoughts all along the way?

TOMMIE: I'd like to say all the way. He imprinted in me a way of looking at things, that anything is possible if you want it enough. I was really affected when I learned he had died—stronger than I expected.

ARAM: What was it about him?

TOMMIE: He was, in a way, my introduction to music played not from a record but live. Apart from Lennart Annemark, he was the first musician I really saw play with burning conviction. The first time he showed me a C-major chord on the guitar, I practiced for a whole week just to master that chord. Hours a day, learning that chord and how to switch to another chord. And when I came up with the idea that I wanted to write music in the style of the classics, he taught me harmony, function, how to set up an orchestral score, rhythm and hearing exercises, and so on. He took me so seriously. Who would suggest a fifteen-year-old arrange and conduct Beethoven's Ninth to be performed by the school's orchestra? What I learned later from my next guitar teacher, Bo Strömberg, was that you had to put bone-hard effort into it, but Claes-Göran was more into music for the joy of it, and that was so important then.

ARAM: Were you in touch with Claes-Göran throughout the years?

TOMMIE: No, we didn't hear from each other for many, many years. When I started to be more established, we had some contact

Photo: Per Löfsvedn

Tommie Haglund with Claes-Göran Bjerding at Hagby Church, ca. 1982.

on the phone. He visited me in Halmstad a couple of times. The last time was a weekend in the spring of 2001. Two days earlier, I had fallen on the lawn and broken my foot in two places. I didn't realize it was broken, and I walked on it for two days. Elisabet was gone, and Claes-Göran had to take me to the emergency room, where we sat for hours. I told him about my childhood and wondered how he perceived me. He told me a lot about himself, too. Many years later, he came to a performance of my cello concerto with Ernst Simon Glaser, and he was so proud. The last time we saw each other was in 2017. He came to Karlskrona for a premier of a piece I wrote for violin and piano. I was so glad and surprised to see him. We were talking, and he reminded me of something I'd said during a radio interview. He remembered me saying that the last thing I'd ever want to hear about my music was that it was entertaining. But he said, "Tommie, when I heard 'La Rosa Profunda Alborada' today, I *was* entertained!" I took the opportunity to thank him for all the things he had given me. The week after, he died suddenly in his sleep.

2: SMÖRGÅSBORD

ARAM: Going back to your younger years, after your visit to the hospital, your experiences with music were, you said, very limited. Maybe pop music and Mozart. But after this, you were brought into contact with more work by classical composers. I believe Vivaldi was one of them.

TOMMIE: Absolutely. Vivaldi was a radio discovery, also in the car, with the whole family. I was probably the only one listening. The rest were talking. You see, there were three state radio channels. There was no commercial radio in Sweden until 1990. Radio-P1 was talk radio, news, science, analysis, that kind of stuff. Radio-P2 was classical music and maybe foreign-language news. And Radio-P3 was, in those days, popular music, sports, variety programs. You could have Swedish folk accordion music, the Beatles, classical, a complete mix.

ARAM: Smörgåsbord.

TOMMIE: It was actually like a smörgåsbord! And it wasn't all focused on commercial music. In the middle of this, on Radio-3, they played Vivaldi's Concerto in C Major—you know, with piccolo, string orchestra, flute, and harpsichord—they played only the slow movement of it. I thought it was so beautiful, so immensely beautiful. High notes, singing like a bird, hitting all the right notes that created this solitary atmosphere. It just broke me. I had to bite my lip to keep my composure. I'll never forget that moment. I remember after it had finished, the announcer told me it was by a gentleman named Antonio Vivaldi, and I thought, who is he? Where does he live? I've got to write to him or something and thank him for this immense beauty. I wanted to know what he did to create this poetry. How did he do it? Later, when I had a chance to buy the record and play the chords on my guitar, I realized it was all about clever modulations combined with a fantastic way of making melodies that went straight into me. This melancholy combined with sincere beauty.

ARAM: Was that your very first purchased classical record?

TOMMIE: No, my first record was some sort of mixed album with highlights of Beethoven, Bach, Rimsky-Korsakov. I've got it downstairs. It was Bach's Brandenburg Concerto No. 4 or 5, I believe. I did also have a record of Vivaldi. Beethoven I studied really severely when I was young. I read about his life and listened to his symphonies 3, 5, 7, and 9, and the late quartets. He made a tremendous impact on me.

ARAM: Beethoven's late quartets had an impact?

TOMMIE: Oh yes, yes. Beethoven was a cornerstone.

ARAM: What was the first music you studied on your own?

TOMMIE: Music from the Baroque struck me first, but also Schubert's Symphony No. 4—the *Tragic*. My grandparents on my mother's side had an old recording with Sir Adrian Boult conducting, and I also loved listening to Alfvén's *Midsommarvaka,* a piece I then thought was very inventive, almost like film music. That was also an old recording.

ARAM: What else?

TOMMIE: Mozart, Marcello, and a few minor things by Grieg. Especially their slow movements, when they were taking their time. It captivated me. And sometimes, they had these unexpected harmonies and melodies, particularly with Bach. I listened to the way he treated harmonies and counterpoint in the Brandenburg Concertos—changing chords almost on every beat. I thought it was fantastic and liberating, really. I learned so much from listening to that. But I still wanted to know who these people were who wrote such wild things. I read every biography I could get hold of. Also, of historical figures like Napoleon and Charles XII of Sweden, who ruled when these composers were living and working, to have a grip on the context in which they worked. And elephants. I wanted to know all about them, how they could feel vibrations in the ground miles away, and how they mourned the dead. I made connections between them and these composers—their abilities to hear and feel vibrations in the ground. I read so many of these romantic books about Beethoven with exaggerated intrigues. Many of the composers lived hard lives and suffered. And I thought, if that's what it costs, I think it's worth the price.

ARAM: What was the first piece you recorded?

TOMMIE: Baroque trumpet and organ. You'll hear lots of Vivaldi, that kind of thing. [*Plays a recording of Allegro, Opus 1.*]

ARAM: You weren't kidding about the Baroque trumpet.

TOMMIE: I was so young.

ARAM: Could be used in a graduation ceremony. It was reminiscent of something . . .

TOMMIE: Yes, everything!

ARAM: Terrific for eleven. What did your parents think?

TOMMIE: They must have been proud to see me in the newspaper, but beyond that, they didn't take it very seriously.

ARAM: The trumpet arrangement was joyous.

TOMMIE: Not at all how I felt at the time.

ARAM: How were you feeling?

TOMMIE: A mixture of worry and curiosity. And I had a lot of anxiety.

ARAM: At eleven?

TOMMIE: We lived in Kalmar until, it must have been, 1969. I had been back at school from the hospital for one whole year, and then, we moved out from town, half an hour or so by car, to a place—as I felt—out in the country, to a village called Trekanten. It was really way out in the sticks. I used to take my bike into Kalmar—it took an hour at least—to a record shop and listen to the opening fugue of Bach's B-Minor Mass.

ARAM: You listened to it in the shop?

TOMMIE: Yes, in the shop. You could do that with headphones in those days. And then, I rode back again with the music ringing in my ears. I couldn't buy the record. I had no money to burn. The B-Minor Mass combined knife-sharp intellect with a daring harmony—everything so expressive. When it was tense at home, I felt solace being among the great composers. This was also the time I studied with Claes-Göran. I remember one Sunday afternoon, I was perhaps twelve, and I heard something symphonic in my head and wanted to orchestrate it, but I didn't know how to do it. I phoned Claes-Göran, and he said, "Come over for a couple of hours if someone can drive you." No one wanted to drive me, so I took my younger brother's minibike and cycled the 30 kilometers to his little cottage in Vassmolösa, and then he drove me back. Composing was so important, and I felt anything else would have been a waste of time. Not that I was looking down on people working in shops or whatever, but I couldn't see myself doing that.

ARAM: You just couldn't see yourself doing something routine.

TOMMIE: I couldn't see myself sitting in an office. I was active in many areas when I was in high school. I was the chairman of the student council, and I was on the board of the Swedish Student National Union. And I played table tennis. When I was thirteen, I started a rock band, and we played at many school dance parties. I wanted that full-on electric guitar force. And you could get girls. I remember once when I was playing, there were lots of girls standing and watching us, and I lost my pick, so I had to play with my fingers. I don't know how long I played, but when I looked down, there was blood smeared everywhere. I hadn't noticed. What I liked about rock music was the mixture of life force and fury, in particular, played by a really tight band. After a while, it felt too one-dimensional. I wanted a fuller spectrum sound that allowed sometimes for a softer voice.

ARAM: Who else was in the band?

TOMMIE: Oh, there was a drummer from Stockholm, Bo Holstein. There was also Ulf Wikström; he has his own company in Kalmar. Another who works in a music shop; he was a good soloist. Dag Lundberg was the only one who went further with music. What united us, apart from the music, was our love for the absurd comedy we used to play out on each other.

ARAM: That was a time when so much was happening here in Sweden—psychedelic and prog bands playing all night. I don't suppose the band you were playing in had these leftist ambitions or that you wanted to feel a part of that festival scene.

TOMMIE: No, absolutely not. I've always had difficulty with ideology and -isms. They castrate the art. The leftist bands that combined political text with country and western music just didn't interest me. They ended up sounding mediocre very quickly.

That aversion had its roots in a car journey that my family and I made to Italy in 1971. We were to drive through the DDR (*Deutsche Demokratische Republik*, German Democratic Republic), and of course, I had heard about the communist dictatorships. But the shock I experienced when the ferry arrived in Sassnitz was unforgettable. The first thing I saw was soldiers with Kalashnikovs and a country that hadn't changed since the war. When we walked the streets of East Berlin, elderly people came up eager to tell us how trapped they were and how tormented they felt, and they hoped that we would take this information back to Sweden. It was awful. I remember vividly how carefully they looked around themselves to make sure they weren't being watched. My dad happened to drive the wrong way in Potsdam, and right away, we were stopped by three cars, and out came armed police officers, one pointing a machine gun through the window. They must have seen the three frightened kids in the back seat—my siblings and me. We saw barbed wire all over the border and watchtowers with armed guards so that people wouldn't escape. It was like coming into an evil dream! The contrast when we returned to West Berlin was unbelievable.

We read a lot in the papers about the fascist dictators in Spain and Greece, but we rarely heard about the communists in the East. I always sympathized with the underdog, but this was the total opposite for me. I got furious at the so-called communists in Kalmar who spoke openly about Mao, Che Guevara, and Lenin. If you pointed out the mass murders these people left in their wake, these communists just said either that it was necessary or that wasn't their idea of communism. I simply couldn't understand why they wanted to change the society we lived in.

There was one of these leftist prog bands in Kalmar called Ragnarök, and there were things they did that appealed to me, but they never had that swinging beat, that trance. Their music was very intricate, but it wasn't what *I* thought of as rock. I was listening to [John] Dowland[3] a lot in those days, and I see a relation in a way with rock music. Dowland had the same sort of darkness you can find in some rock music. I think he would have been a good rock musician in another time or would have liked that sort of music. But many of his subtle and painfully beautiful melodies can't be contained in the rock idiom.

ARAM: I thought the same thing about Rameau when we listened to the overture to *Acante et Céphise*. But yes, there is a real angst in Dowland.

---

3 John Dowland (1563–1626) was an English Renaissance composer and lutenist known best for his strikingly melancholic song cycles, which were an important inspiration to Haglund.

TOMMIE: Oh, yes, there were affinities to Dowland in how I felt. I often felt worried and powerless as I was growing up. This laid the groundwork for my music. A mixture of melancholy and lightning strikes of worry and a terrible fear of dying. The thought that everything was to end, and that I was not even to remember that I had lived. That feeling terrified me. I would lie awake. Why was I born if I had to die? Why couldn't God spare us the torment?

I didn't have many close friends. The ones I had were very close. For example, I had my friend Per Löfsveden, who carried in him the same kind of craziness I did, like the subversion of the Monty Python crew. When we were twelve or thirteen, we wanted to get back at this fellow who had told us off—probably for a good reason. He owned a big house, and we snuck out at night with shovels and completely re-landscaped his entire yard! We moved every shrub. We did a great job and even used measuring tape—just to confuse him. It was that kind of creative madness that lights up life in the countryside.

ARAM: [*Laughs.*] Did you ever write pop music?

TOMMIE: Per and I used to write Simon and Garfunkel-inspired tunes, which we played and sang at small gatherings. Very naïve lyrics. I figured out how to improvise. I discovered Status Quo and Creedence Clearwater Revival with John Fogerty, who had a voice filled with masculine power and pain.

ARAM: If Beethoven were alive today, what would he be listening to and writing himself?

TOMMIE: I think he would feel flattered, considering rock guitar riffing is, to a certain extent, a direct follow-up to his way of using short motifs. Emotionally, I'm sure he would have sympathized with the energy and power. He certainly would have found something to shake us up with humanism and protest.

ARAM: There is an immediacy to rock n' roll that punk rock distilled down further.

TOMMIE: The punk era was a liberation—very refreshing. It removed the pretentious symphonic rock and Swedish left-wing bands like Hoola Bandoola and Blå Tåget. I'm fascinated by music where I can't sit still. It's a very primitive feeling. I was listening to John Fogerty the other day—a live concert—and sometimes he really gets it. Suddenly, you have that pulse, like he's in contact with eternity. I have great respect for musicians who can create that irresistible sound.

3: THE GUITAR

ARAM: How did you meet your second guitar teacher, Bo Strömberg?

TOMMIE: When I was in high school. I was fifteen. They used to have a system where students got two weeks during the school year to visit a workplace. I was thinking of being a music teacher, so I went with Claes-Göran Bjerding to Kommunala Musikskolan.[4] They had a pedagogical meeting when they gathered all the music teachers, and there was Bo Strömberg. I met him and thought he was very charismatic and self-assured. I realized right away he played the guitar with a different technique than I had ever seen before. But I hadn't heard much classical guitar at that time. So, I met him later on in a restaurant at the City Hotel in Kalmar, and I dared to approach and ask if I could have a lesson. "Yes, of course! Bring literature with you," he said. Literature? What does he mean by that? Printed music? I didn't have any. Anyway, I played "Spanish

4 Kommunala Musikskolan is the municipal music school.

Romance"—in the wrong key, which he pointed out immediately. He put me on a chair with a footstool for classical players and rearranged my hands, and I couldn't play. You see, Claes-Göran was largely self-taught and never talked about hand position, but Bo studied classical guitar with Hector Quine[5] in London. Bo was baffled because I'd learned everything by ear, but not in quite the right way, you know? I had to relearn everything, but it was a very good experience to focus on technique. I told him that I composed, and he said, "Composing is just paperwork. I'll make you a brilliant guitarist!" So, I embraced that. And he gave me technique studies, the old classical methods: Fernando Sor, Francisco Tarrega, Matteo Carcassi, and some from a method that Bo himself was working on. It was based partly on what he learned in private lessons with Hector Quine. Bo wrote five method books between 1978 and 1981 or so, and at the time, they were the most thorough and ambitious guitar method published in Sweden.

Sometimes, I didn't bring the music with me because I knew it, and that made him frustrated—which I understand—but I think it amused him as well. So, he arranged for me to play concerts. We played a guitar trio, myself and two girls. And we actually played on Swedish television once. Soon I got to be well-known in the area as a guitarist—strange to look back on that.

But to go back to my first lesson with Bo, my strongest memory—it was like a revelation—was when he had me listen to Julian Bream and John Williams. The first thing he played me was a duo record, but that didn't appeal to me at all. It was music by Carulli.

---

5 Hector Quine (1926–2015) was a well-known English guitar teacher and a teacher at the Royal Academy of Music.

I thought it was ridiculous, pling-plong-pling-plong, aimless. But then Bo played a record of Bream when he played English Renaissance music by Dowland on the lute. We talked about Dowland before. It's difficult to explain what in the music woke up such emotional memories. It was almost as if this music had been in me all along. What we heard was a solo piece for the lute, "Semper Dowland, semper dolens."

I continued taking lessons from Bo at the Kommunala Musikskolan in Kalmar. After a term, I found the courage to say it was the music of Dowland and the Renaissance that I wanted to go into deeper. So, he lent me lots of these records, mostly lute music but also chamber music with the Julian Bream Consort.

Bo was very generous. He didn't charge for the extra lessons before I was to play a concert. I occasionally even had lessons with him on the weekends when he was supposed to be free. He was serious about music, and it was not always fun to have a lesson with him—it was sometimes stress-inducing. Once at a concert I sat on the stage, dead nervous. And where was he? I was to play a piece by Mauro Giuli and one of my own compositions. And there was Bo, way in the back, covering his face with his hands, even more nervous than I was. But it was because he took his work as a teacher so seriously. He had great stamina, sometimes to the brink of exhaustion—real perseverance. My way of working with a piece of music for a very long time came from that. It also meant a lot that I could talk to him about how it was at home—problems with my parents.

ARAM: And what happened when you finally moved out of your parents' house?

TOMMIE: As I mentioned before, my father and I never got along. I was the oldest child and probably the reason they were married at nineteen. It shocked my father's parents, who saw the pregnancy as a scandal. Perhaps my arrival got in the way of things my father would have liked to do with his life other than suddenly becoming a parent. Gradually, his relationship with alcohol came to be destructive. It couldn't have been easy for either of them. My mom did what she could to keep the family together. But as time went by, it just got worse.

I remember a Saturday evening when I was sixteen. For some reason, my dad was laying into me, and I realized it was going to get physical. Outside, it was -20°C, but I had finally had enough and rushed out the door in my socks and no jacket and ran more than a mile to a phone box. I couldn't feel my feet. I had one coin and phoned Bo, who lived in Kalmar, which was nine miles further on. He said, "Take a taxi, and I'll pay for it. You can stay here for the night." I'll never forget him for that. Meanwhile, the police were organizing a search because my parents thought I had frozen to death. I phoned them late the next afternoon and said to my father, "If you ever hit me, you'll never see me again." And it stopped. But I had to leave Kalmar to survive mentally. A couple of years later, Bo moved to Halmstad to teach at the Kommunala Musikskolan there. He helped me get a job teaching guitar thirteen hours a week. I was eighteen and rented a room in the same area—near where we are now (Sofiabacken neighborhood, Halmstad). It was a room in a basement: space enough for a bed, a small chair, and a TV set on the wall. I think it was 200 kronor a month. The house was owned by some well-to-do couple. I started there with nothing.

Photo: Tommie Haglund

Bo Strömberg, ca. 1980

ARAM: This was 1977?

TOMMIE: Yes.

ARAM: How long did you stay in that room?

TOMMIE: Only a few months. Bo got a divorce, so I moved in with him because I lived frugally, almost in poverty. That was the start of one of the periods in my life when I felt I had no solid ground under me.

ARAM: More so than living with your parents?

TOMMIE: There were some bright moments. Mainly, it was the fact that I had just moved from home for the first time, didn't have a proper job, and was at the mercy of Bo. We were both in a mess. I was sleeping in the TV room, and at eight o'clock every morning, he woke me up, which I hated, and he made me practice. My girlfriend Helen was supposed to move from Kalmar to Lund to study Latin. We only corresponded by letters and longed for each other. Bo suggested I spend more time practicing, and that meant less time with Helen, who lived two hours away. Finally, the situation became unbearable, and she got a job at Högskolan i Halmstad (Halmstad University) and we moved in together.

ARAM: Did you do anything else at that time besides teach and practice?

TOMMIE: To get away from things, Bo and I used to go to Hovs Hallar, where Ingmar Bergman filmed the chess scene from *The Seventh Seal.* I wasn't used to climbing cliffs for hours like that. It was like washing my brain clean by the open sea. Bo used to take photos with his Leica and develop them in the closet.

One day a week, I taught guitar at Holm, which was four miles away, and when I finished at 9 p.m., there was no bus home, so Bo came to pick me up in the car. It was very kind of him to take such responsibility for me. After a while, he started the guitar society here, which he did by gathering his best students in Halmstad. It grew to be open to guitarists from all over Scandinavia. It was called Apoyando, which is a technical term for a certain way of hitting the strings.

We had many classical guitar concerts there in the town gallery, every month, in fact, with all sorts of programming. We played trios, quartets, and solo pieces. We had a magazine called *Cadenza,* where, apart from serious articles, I acted as the Guitar Man in a kind of comic strip of photos. It was a parody of *The Phantom.* It started with me coming out of the sea in a perambulator. Bo was dressed up as an old Greek, and so on. That society was where I met my friend Sven Dymne, who was the first one to tell me about Swedenborg.

ARAM: Even before Soldanella?

TOMMIE: Yes, that's right. Sven had seen something on the television or something like that. I just went, "Yeah-yeah, another dry Swedish academic." It's funny with Sven. He's the root of so many things.

ARAM: Did you play concerts with Sven?

TOMMIE: No, he had no ambitions even to be a musician, just a music teacher, and he has great musical knowledge. I think by then, he had started to study to be a teacher in either Gothenburg or Malmö. He had this mad sense of humor that suited me perfectly, and he wrote absurd poems and said very strange things. He lived with his mother on the other side of the river in a very small flat. She was half-deaf and paralyzed. Sven had taken care of her since he was thirteen. I remember that when I went to his flat for the first time, I saw all these decorations in the window—skulls, the same paper cut-out technique they use in kindergartens, but skulls instead of little trees or whatever. We got together to listen to music often. And our children are the same age. You know, the paradox is that he belongs to the largest extended family in the world, and yet he himself had none. His father died long ago, and his mother just after I met him.

Part Two

Vision

4: LONDON

ARAM: I'm interested in the early guitar pieces you composed.

TOMMIE: The first was "Aforismer." Bo Strömberg suggested the title, and at that point, he suggested I study with Sune Smedeby.[6] It was my first fumbling attempt at musical modernism, that piece. I had a record by Julian Bream with guitar music from the 1970s, and I was fascinated by his ability to transform this rather inaccessible music into something exciting. It encouraged me to go out of the tonal world and find a new language. "Aforismer" was a sort of theme and variation of a melody. Bo suggested I send it to the composer Per Lindgren in Stockholm—he was a former student of Bo's—and he replied briefly, encouraging me to go on and write more.

ARAM: What were your thoughts on what you wanted to do, musically, beyond the guitar?

---

6 Sune Smedeby (1934–1998) was a Swedish composer and author of books on music theory.

TOMMIE: I had an urge to read all I could find about Beethoven, Bach, and Dowland—scores, biographies, to learn as much as possible. Julian Bream inspired me a lot at this time. I'm mainly thinking of his way of playing Dowland—it's almost demonic. His importance for the guitar in the twentieth century was like Horowitz was for the piano, with an expressive virtuosity far beyond technique. Segovia doesn't even get close, in my opinion. There was something about Dowland's music that went straight to my heart. He expressed sadness, joy, and longing far beyond words. I tried to compose similarly but didn't yet have a language of my own. Then, I met John Mills, the English guitarist, who lived in London. Bream said about his sound that it was England's most beautiful tone. That meeting with John and his striving to achieve this beautiful sound changed my direction.

ARAM: You went to London to meet John?

TOMMIE: No, he came to visit Halmstad to teach a master class. He was invited by Apoyando and paid for by the ABF.[7] All the guitarists in Halmstad participated, including several of Bo's students. I played Fernando Sor's "Variations on a Theme by Mozart." Lots of guitarists from Scandinavia were there listening. I was dead nervous and didn't consider myself to be very good. But Mills came up afterward and said, "I think you should come to one of my master classes at Burton Manor."

7 ABF (Arbetarnas Bildningsförbund) was a study association for adults and children strongly supported by the Swedish Social Democratic Party. Its goal was to make education available to union members, but anyone could sign up for the courses, which were mostly held in the evenings.

Photo: Tommie Haglund

John Mills, ca. 1983

ARAM: Was it a shock that John Mills came up to you saying this?

TOMMIE: It really was. Someone playing in a manner I had never heard before. So much poetry and beauty, but also a bit wild and unrestrained.

ARAM: So, you went to Burton Manor in Cheshire prior to living in London? What was that like?

TOMMIE: Yes, I flew into Manchester. John turned up at the airport in a big blue Japanese car with four female guitar students in it. I sat with them in the back seat all the way to Burton Manor. I'd been to London before, but not to the rest of England. It's idyllic and old-fashioned. I felt very at home there, particularly with the people. The master classes were very interesting and of the highest quality, but the evening concerts were more like variety shows, with professional and amateur participants on the stage at the same time. It was so liberating to be in a context where jokes and seriousness were mixed—so English. There was one very good American guitarist, Scott Saari, and a Dutch guitarist, Cobie Smit, who was later to become John's wife; there was a zookeeper named Frank and a computer engineer named Steven—they were amateur guitarists. The amateurs laughed at themselves. Frank read poems—typical English humor with great conviction that I loved. And there were three elderly ladies on the stage, trying to play through *Elizabethan Serenade* arranged for a guitar trio. They had to stop all the time, and the audience roared with laughter and almost fell off their chairs. I also took lessons in baroque interpretation with Evelyn Nallen, who is a renowned recorder player. John's humor was very much like Monty Python. I wanted to communicate music the same way he did, with great depth but also relaxed and free. I realized also what a perfectionist he could be in a way I'd never seen before. The next step for me, I realized, was to arrange to study with John in London.

ARAM: Did Helen go with you to London?

TOMMIE: No, she stayed here. She had a job with the university. We briefly thought of moving to England, but there was great unemployment in England during the Thatcher years. I went to the bank and took a loan for a sum that could keep me going a while. You could do that in those days. John said, "Well, you can be put up in something called the Cedars Guesthouse" in Kingston, close to Long Ditton, where he lived. It was owned by Lord William

Townsend—generally called Bill. He was a huge fellow, very kind, walking about in a worn-out sweater, living in a little room with a bed and a TV. But he owned a big mansion outside of town and a green Jaguar. He couldn't stand his wife, so he ran the guesthouse during the week. He roomed with a little, retired sea captain named Don Christie, who probably lived there for free. He was 70 or 75 and loved strong curries. They both loved classical guitar music.

ARAM: What did they think of you as a Swede?

TOMMIE: You know the English. They're obsessed with class, at least in a way that's alien to Swedes. So, after a few days of living there, Bill asked about my parents and their background. I told him, well, my father worked for NOHAB, the company that installed the Swedish press system for *The Daily Telegraph* and *Financial Times*. Dad went over there for a year or two to supervise in the late 1970s. "Where did he live?" they asked. "St. John's Wood," I said. "Ahh," he said, "that's a top-notch place." So, I was instantly one of his own. Stupid, but that's how they adopted me.

Most of the time, it was easy to get along with Bill and Don Christie, and I could see that they wanted to help me with practical matters. One Christmas, Helen and I ran the guesthouse while Bill and Don went abroad. But I couldn't stay there the whole time. It would be too expensive, and Bill didn't have any other estates in the city, but he knew people who did. "So," he said, "Why don't you get elected into the Conservative Club?"

"OK, how will that happen since I'm Swedish?"

"Well," he said, "you phone the Conservative Party in Sweden," which was the Moderata Samlingspartiet, "become a member of that, and they send the form over here." So, I phoned and joined the Conservative Party! I had them send something to the Tories, and I became a member of the Conservative Club in Kingston. I went there; it was an aristocratic sort of place. I met the fellow who owned the houses. “I’ll put you up,” he said. “I’ve got a big room you can hire with a kitchen.” I shared the toilet with a lot of people, and I had to put coins in a machine to get heating every day. England was so backward in those days! And in a way, it still is. You’d come home from the pub in the winter and just drop, and in the morning, oh no, you’ve forgotten to put the coins in, and it was freezing. You could see your breath. But there I lived and practiced. There was this old-fashioned dining table in the middle of the room, and at night, I had to take the cushions from the dining chairs and put them under the bed mattress; otherwise it would collapse, and I’d fall out. But none of this bothered me at all. It allowed me to do what I loved.

ARAM: So, by this time, you had started lessons with John.

TOMMIE: Yes, when I arrived in London to have the first lesson with John, we played together, and he said, “Come on, set yourself free, and don’t be afraid of making mistakes.” He was in his thirties then and was living at home with his parents because he was traveling so much. We became lifelong friends. I think the reason we connected on so many different levels was that we shared this romantic, old-fashioned attitude about music and an absurd sense of humor.

When he was touring around England, I traveled with him, and we played together. We went out with these eccentric characters, people you can only meet in England. I met one guy from New Zealand who hated the British system; his name was Fred McEwen.

This was the Thatcher era, as I mentioned. The Falklands had just ended. They had invented the Harrier jet in the sixties—you know, the plane that could take off and land vertically. Fred worked at the factory where they made them. I used to see him at the pub in the evenings. "You should see these planes," he said. "You should see the interior. There is a big hangar where they have them cut in half so you can see through all the workings." "I can't get in there," I said, "I'd be considered a spy." "No, no," he said, "I'll get you in. You can borrow my brown coat and a cap, and then you buy a pork pie in plastic. You take the bus up to the factory and go to the entrance where the workers come in. You go there at 12 o'clock when they have their lunch. When they go out, you go in, and I'll go with you." I got in there, but it was dangerous; there were a lot of people. We went into this enormous hangar with glass walls, and behind the glass, there were people supervising or whatever, but they were eating. So, we got into the hangar and went up a ladder and could look at these planes. Fantastic construction, all these tubes. I didn't understand anything. Had I been an engineer or spy, I could have photographed everything.

I met so many other strange characters in those days—people from the aristocracy, people who had been in the Second World War. The elderly gentleman who took my room when I was to go home had been in the war as a bomber pilot. He invited me back once he had moved in. He was the stereotype for the old British military, and now the only thing he did was paint. I expected to see something pastoral or some portraits, but instead, the walls were covered with paintings of bombing raids. I could only guess what went on in the old man's head.

Photo: Tommie Haglund

Outdoor view of the residence at Cranes Park, Surbiton Hill, UK, ca. 1983, one of multiple residences Tommie inhabited.

ARAM: All of this was while you were studying with John?

TOMMIE: Yes, I studied with John every week unless he was on tour abroad. And always at the end of the lesson, the door opened, and you'd see two hands with a tray, and on the tray, there was tea with apple pie and custard. That was John's mum, and it signaled the end of the lesson, and then he'd put on these 78 rpm discs. He had an entire wall covered with them, most in mint condition. He'd play some, and I realized music was made in a very different way than the way we are making it now. When the 78 rpm discs were made, it was a single take. Rhythmically, they were so free and fiery. It was there that I first heard the music of Delius.

ARAM: At some point, did you decide you would compose seriously for more than just guitar?

TOMMIE: Oh yes. When I heard Delius' music, I realized I would not be a guitarist. Delius' sound world was an invitation to start composing again after being totally focused on playing the guitar. We had dinner in my flat for John and his then-to-be wife, Cobie Smit. And he brought a cassette with a recording of the 78 rpm disc, the Pougnet-Beecham recording. The batteries in my tape recorder were low, but John was so insistent that I hear Delius that we went to a petrol station to buy more batteries. I'd never heard music like that in my life, but John really wanted to introduce it to me. He knew this very personal musical language would appeal to me. He even gave me a cigar and a glass of port, and I heard Delius' Violin Concerto from 1916 with the surface noise, which added a layer of mystery to it. Delius was something completely new. When I came to John Mills, a whole new world opened, with romanticism and free feeling, tempo and agogics,[8] and an overwhelming sense of harmony that would have an enormous impact.

ARAM: So, the first time you heard Delius was with John?

TOMMIE: No, actually, I had bought a record when I was eighteen, in Lund. It had Delius' miniatures, but that wasn't why I bought the record. It also had Vaughan Williams' *Lark Ascending* and William Walton's incidental music for a Shakespeare play. That's why I bought the record, but I did listen to Delius' miniatures. *Summer Night on the River* was also there. I found the harmonies a

---

8 Fluctuation of tempo within musical phrasing rather than by increasing dynamic stress.

bit restless, especially compared to Vaughan Williams and Walton, which are like easy listening. The Delius wasn't easy listening. But they were small works, and they didn't tempt me to go further. I didn't know at the time he had written larger-scale works.

ARAM: But the real beginning of your interest in him was actually with Mills.

TOMMIE: Yes, it really was when John Mills played the 78 rpm discs for me in London. I really began paying attention then. I did know who he was, but I didn't know anything about him.

ARAM: What of Delius did you hear with John?

TOMMIE: The Violin Concerto and the opening of the *Song of Summer*, which was taken by dictation to Eric Fenby. I'll never forget my first impression of the D major string chord when the cello and bass played the notes G#-A-D-C. I asked John to dub *North Country Sketches* onto tape and then all the other pieces he had. I wasn't at all disturbed by the surface noise. I think the radio noise from my hospital experience added to the otherworldly feeling.

5: ÅRHUS, DENMARK

ARAM: After you'd moved out of the flat and the bomber pilot had moved in, where did you go?

TOMMIE: I went back to Halmstad for a time and later returned to London for more lessons.

ARAM: What made you decide to go to the conservatory in Denmark?

TOMMIE: Leif Christensen, a professor from the Royal Academy in Århus, put on a concert in Halmstad arranged by Apoyando. He played some very curious and difficult pieces by Giulio Regondi, a nineteenth-century virtuoso—some newly discovered compositions. They didn't say anything much to me, but it's very virtuosic, and it meant a lot to Leif. But there was nothing in Leif's playing that captured the warmth and power that was so natural to John Mills or Julian Bream. Anyway, he stayed with us, and one night, he heard me practice, and he suggested I should come to Århus to study. I wasn't convinced. But then, when I returned from London, I thought, well, I probably won't be accepted, but I'll do this audition and see what level I'm at. I took the ferry across to Århus and played for the jury. I wasn't nervous at all. I just really wanted to get as much sound as I could out of the guitar. It was difficult for foreigners to be admitted to the conservatory because there was a quota system, and you had to beat all the Danes. But I ended up with the highest score!

ARAM: What did you play?

TOMMIE: A very fine composition by John Mills—an homage to Delius, a rather complicated piece, then some Spanish music by Torroba and *Tombeau D'Monsieur Hartig* and *Fantasie* by the baroque composer Silvius Leopold Weiss. All very poetic music. The headmaster of the school came up to me and said in Danish, "Do you want to be a concert guitarist?" I said, "Well, maybe." But then I was a bit upset when I heard from a student that my playing needed to be tamed. It was too wild. But anyway, I just ended up in Århus, a place I never really wanted to be, and I found myself surrounded by guitarists who didn't know anything about symphonic music. They didn't know Mahler and didn't know Tchaikovsky. They knew them as names only.

ARAM: What did they know?

TOMMIE: Standard works for the guitar. Fernando Sor, Walton, Britten, Giuliani, but no music for other instruments. And, of course, a couple of Bach lute suites and the Spanish twentieth-century repertoire.

ARAM: And Rodrigo?

TOMMIE: Yes, Rodrigo. I moved down there, and I couldn't understand a word they were saying. I never understood Danish. I do now. I speak fluently now. So, I moved into a student corridor built in the '70s—very modernistic, concrete walls and needle-felt carpet. There was a big common space with a public kitchen. It was a collectivist, half-socialist situation. There were fourteen of us, so every fourteenth day I bought all the food and cooked for everyone. You had to do that. I didn't want to at first, but this big Danish guy came in and said, "Now listen, you. We're doing it like this here." Those were the rules, so I did it.

ARAM: By this point, you knew you only wanted to compose.

TOMMIE: Yes, I gradually started to question why I was there. I wanted only to compose. So, then I had my first lesson with this Danish teacher, Erling Møldrup. He was a splendid guy—sadly, he died just last year [2016]. He played lots of Per Nørgård, which interested me a great deal, but it wasn't the music of my heart. Møldrup had a solid technique, but self-expression was maybe not his strength. He might as well have been a Swiss watchmaker for the way he performed—a lot of care for details but no sort of romantic elasticity like with John Mills. He loved guitar music more than anything else, you could tell. He could play the most difficult pieces. The first lesson I had with him, he came in and said, "Oh, it's the arch enemy," meaning the wars between Sweden and Denmark in the 1600s. Well, that's a welcome, I thought. But he took to me. I had my lessons at his home. Sometimes, when we were at the Academy, we had a lesson at 10 o'clock in the morning, and after that, we'd go down to the canteen, and he always ordered beef tartare.

ARAM: How were you perceived at the Academy?

TOMMIE: I was considered a very odd person at the Academy. I was interested in 78 rpm discs. I wanted to talk about Mahler,

Photo: Martin Buch

Tommie Haglund with his Volvo PV outside the conservatory's student dormitory, Århus, ca. 1984

Delius, and big orchestral works. They had a fantastic library with all the records you can imagine, but I was the only guitarist in there listening to anything. I didn't fit in. They were all about their fingerings, and there I was, walking around with a cassette of the Delius violin concerto in my pocket. I thought they were very German in their approach—in a negative sense. Very academic, and you were not allowed to express sensuality, wildness, or uncontrolled feelings.

ARAM: Apollo without Dionysus.

TOMMIE: Yes, a castrated Apollo, at least to my taste. [*Laughs.*] It was horrible. Then, I met this cellist, John Ehde, who became a life-changing friend. It was for him that I eventually wrote the cello concerto. He was sitting in this listening room with his followers—he was the star pupil; he was a real Romantic. He played cello and really gave it everything. Anyway, he used to sit in there with a bunch of admirers listening to old recordings with Stokowski. When the music stopped, I asked, "Have you heard Delius?" "Yes, I played his *Brigg Fair* once," he said. "But have you heard this?" I asked and put in the cassette tape with the violin concerto. He sat there, hypnotized. It was the first time I experienced someone listening to music with his whole body. That shook me up—to be completely physically absorbed.

String instrumentalists and pianists, like at the conservatory, saw guitarists as second-rate musicians. But John and I were both Swedes, and we became very good friends. Night after night, we listened to Delius, and we discovered a lot of new works we didn't know. We formed a strong bond, and as I began to grow more distant from the guitarists, I saw more of the violinists, singers, pianists, and cellists—talking with them about what I considered to be the real thing. I learned a lot from them. The guitar music from the 1800s to the early 1900s is mainly pedagogical—written for amateur players or whatever—though there is some music by Sor I really love. I mean, at best, you had Julian Bream encouraging Benjamin Britten and Hans Werner Henze to write for the guitar, but apart from that, you haven't got much for the guitar other than Bach transcriptions and Dowland.

ARAM: So why did you spend so much time playing guitar if it's so limited?

TOMMIE: I loved the sound. It's different from the piano and violin—with a guitar, you have direct contact with the strings.

But I think it was the sound that attracted me, particularly the way Mills played. Master guitar makers used to regularly phone John Mills to try out the sound of new instruments, and he would send me when he couldn't go. Once, I overheard him say to a guitar maker in Norwich, "Tommie sounds just like me, so if you don't mind, I'll send him instead." And I went.

ARAM: It sounds like your discovery of Delius was also the discovery of a new sensuality.

TOMMIE: Yes, so I discovered romantic music, and I attended the composition classes and was really disappointed. It was so academic, so . . . Boulez[9]—the more difficult it sounded, the better. The less you understood, the better. That was my perception of it then, anyway.

ARAM: "Who cares if you listen?"

TOMMIE: Exactly. I thought I saw through all that—not to put myself above it. But, I thought, I want to compose, and if music is purely academic, I don't want to do it. Why am I here? Then, I had this vision and an animated argument with this religious student.

ARAM: Who was that?

TOMMIE: Anne-Christin Strömgren. She was a very gifted pianist. I remember that she played lots of Chopin and other similar music. She helped me a lot because I was quite handicapped with practical things, such as buying food or taking care of myself. If I became nervous or upset, she could calm me down. It was no love

---

9 Pierre Boulez (1925–2016) was a French composer and conductor and a dominant figure in post-war continental music, especially serialism and the avant-garde. Haglund's comment refers to a tendency for his compositions to be dogmatically modernist.

affair, nothing like that, but one evening, she explained to me that she was religious, Christian.

ARAM: What denomination?

TOMMIE: Oh, Lutheran, Swedish Church, I think. It bothered me a bit, and one evening, I started to question her: "What's the point? How can you believe such things just to escape reality . . . ?"

ARAM: What then followed?

TOMMIE: What followed was . . . well, I wouldn't call it a quarrel, but I was very agitated, and then I left. We'd been at her apartment, and I got back late to my own room. I was by the window—there was this big glass wall—and it must have been about 2 o'clock in the morning. I was awake. I was standing up, staring through the window, and it was just black, but I had these things before my eyes. It was like looking up into the sky, and it was as if I were racing from the earth into the heavens, over the treetops. I saw the leaves. It was so vivid, and there was no sound. I remember a very clear blue sky and green leaves, and I was heading up to the sky. I felt that this was something spiritual. Someone or something had talked to me. That was my explanation. So, I just made the decision instantly that I was going to only compose. I'd never heard of hypnagogic states. I didn't know what that was. I thought I was going mad or something. It lasted for about fifteen or twenty minutes. But I wasn't afraid. I was just fascinated, and I wondered what was going on. I thought then, there is a God, and he was telling me not to go on as I was anymore and that there is another reality you have no idea about . . . or maybe you have, but you're sort of dismissing it all the time. That's how I interpreted it then. I wouldn't describe it as an utterly religious experience, but I could have become a religious fanatic as a result. I might have felt I'd been "saved" or started to talk about God everywhere I went, but I didn't. I kept it to myself. It really shook me. It really shook me. I admitted to myself, OK, there most likely is a God, and there is certainly another reality. And that was what Anne-Christin had been trying to say to me all night while we argued. And it was that night I decided to go back to Sweden and do what I needed to do—to compose. I stopped being a guitarist. I packed my bags. Straight after the vision faded, I went to the closet and packed everything I owned. I took the train to Grenå in the morning, then the ferry over to Varberg, and then the train to Halmstad. It seems radical, but that's how strong the vision was.

ARAM: During that experience, were you seeing deeper into yourself or deeper into the external world?

TOMMIE: Both. It was an interior journey, but it felt like I was traveling physically toward the sky. So, it was both interior and exterior. I was awake. My eyes were opened. I wasn't going to sleep or anything.

ARAM: At the time, you were anti- or un-religious.

TOMMIE: Yes, at the time, I was very anti-religious, but I think that was just verbally. I was very Delian, very Nietzschean. We're all vegetables.

ARAM: By this time, you'd made the connection between Delius and Nietzsche?

TOMMIE: Yes. That was Nietzsche speaking. It wasn't really me. It was Nietzsche speaking.

ARAM: What year did you leave the conservatory?

TOMMIE: I think 1985.

ARAM: You'd already been writing music for about a decade by this time?

TOMMIE: Yes, I tried to compose, but it didn't come to much of anything. I didn't believe in myself. I didn't believe I had any ability to write with substance. I didn't believe anyone would care to look at it. I found it embarrassing. I didn't want to approach a real musician to look at my work. I felt I wasn't schooled enough to write it seriously.

ARAM: The irony of your fleeing the conservatory in order to dedicate your life to composing music won't be lost on anyone.

TOMMIE: [*Laughs.*] Anyway, I arrived home and woke Helen up. I came into the house in the morning—she didn't know I was coming. I really scared her. She wondered what had happened. I told her I just wanted to compose. I'd almost finished the studies, but I couldn't do it anymore.

ARAM: What was her reaction?

TOMMIE: She was supportive in a way. I said I'd go to the evening school and see if they would hire me to teach guitar.

ARAM: Where was this? Which institution?

TOMMIE: Here, in Halmstad. You see, here in Sweden, they have these evening classes. They're for everyone at the Studiefrämjandet.[10] You could learn English, German, French, piano, guitar, hunting, anything. And I think if you could gather five people, you could get money from the state. All the big political parties had their own schools. There are different organizations running

10 Studiefrämjandet is a study association supported by, among many others, the Farmers Association and Nature Preservation Society. Its charter is politically and religiously neutral.

them: political groups, religious groups, and so on, but they're all non-profit. So, I went to one of those schools, and I knew a woman named Gunilla Inger, so she hired me. I'd start teaching at half past four in the afternoon and work till 10, teaching mostly elderly ladies to play "Tom Dooley," that sort of thing. Bo Strömberg and I had published a guitar teaching method with these sorts of tunes. We were starting a publishing company, he and I. We got it off the ground, but it faded out because it was impossible to earn a living selling guitar music.

6: THE MEDIUM

Compositions: Notturno

ARAM: You and Helen were married before you even left for London, is that right?

TOMMIE: Yes. Helen and I were married in 1981.

ARAM: Who was Helen?

TOMMIE: We met when we were thirteen or fourteen. I fell in love with her. She was sweet, silent, and a bit introverted—which made me curious—and she got very high grades in school. I was much more outgoing and not particularly interested in school achievements. Her main interest was not music, but she supported me in every way, and we needed each other. She was the daughter of an Estonian refugee who came on a raft when the Russians took the Baltic region. He hated the Russians, hated everything red. He had moved out into the forest. You see, he was to become a doctor but had to escape in the middle of his education. He was convinced he'd been followed by the communists, so he hid in the forest at first. For the rest of his life, he made his living in a small community called Påryd, working in a factory where they made yo-yos. He was highly intelligent and a member of the Linnaeus Society. He could read in Latin, German, and English. And he considered me to be some half-communist, disorganized person until he saw what I did. Then he said, "You're like me." That was the best thing he could say. [*Laughs.*] He liked a challenge. Once, when I had to give a lecture on the Brazilian composer Villa-Lobos, he translated an entire biography from German for me. Helen's mother was one of the kindest people you could ever meet, very friendly.

ARAM: When were your children born?

TOMMIE: My first daughter, Victoria, was born in 1985, and Amanda was born in 1988. I have two stepdaughters, Julia and Clara, who were born in 1984 and 1986, but they didn't come into my life until later.

ARAM: What was Helen doing at the time you returned to Sweden?

TOMMIE: She was working at the university administration. We didn't see much of each other. I took care of our daughter, Victoria, in the daytime, taught guitar in the late afternoon and evening, and at nighttime composed. Page after page, writing music, music, music, music, trying to find my way, which I didn't. There were so many obstacles. I couldn't find a language that was really me. It was imitations of different styles—Janáček, Delius, Scriabin, whatever.

ARAM: Did you know then that you should be imitating others to find yourself?

TOMMIE: No. If there's anything I can recommend it's to imitate. Whether it's text, music, or anything else, imitate and study the things you like and that have moved you. Try and recreate them.

That's not stealing. Finally, your own voice will find its place. Take a piece and study until it no longer moves you. Only then can you see how it's constructed.

Bo Strömberg and I played duets and concerts together on a regular basis. I really enjoyed it, but finally, it faded out. After a time, even Bo got fed up with the classical guitar and gave it up, at least for a while. He has always loved jazz, so he started taking lessons from a renowned Swedish jazz guitarist, Ewen Svensson. He also conducted his guitar orchestra called Alhambra at the music school. They traveled all over Europe. I was very impressed about Bo taking lessons from the jazz guitarist, but everything he did was 100 percent, and I like people with that view on life.

Anyway, then I met up with this theater director, Hans Bärtilzon. He later became the chief director of the State Theater in Riga. In the early '80s I had written music for some of the plays he was directing, among them Strindberg's *Ghost Sonata* and Brecht's *The Good Person of Szechwan*. We started talking about Delius, and together, we watched Ken Russell's *Song of Summer*, which is based on Fenby's book. "Wow," he said, "Why don't we do a play about this?" In those days, I was still obsessed with Delius' life and music.

ARAM: You didn't write any music between 1981 and 1987?

TOMMIE: Oh, I wrote music, but I threw most of it away. Just stuff to develop myself. There's lots of unfinished stuff—nothing I'd consider publishing. I found some of them last time I cleaned up the basement. I was surprised by how much there was.

ARAM: There was also *Notturno*, the piece for guitar and flute. A piece in which, honestly, I couldn't locate anything of you.

TOMMIE: Oh yes, that piece was just a step toward something that was not at all clear to me. I wrote *Notturno* when I returned from Århus. Bo told me he'd picked out the five best guitarists from his orchestra and asked me to write a piece for them and a flutist. They played it many times. My guitar teacher from Århus, Erling Møldrup, heard it and phoned me up, and it ended up on a CD he produced.

ARAM: It's interesting that the piece was written just one year before *Intensio Animi*. What a transition occurred in only one year!

TOMMIE: Well, two things happened between *Notturno* and *Intensio Animi*. The first, my oldest daughter, Victoria, was born in 1985. It was the greatest thing that had happened to me. But also, I wondered whether I was up for the task of being a father.

The second thing—I don't know if I can tell you this—but it's a true story; it had a life-changing impact on me, but if people hear this, they'll think I'm soft in the head.

ARAM: Just go ahead.

TOMMIE: I mentioned Sven Dymne before. He has been one of my closest friends since 1978. I expressed to him my despair over my life situation, not having any proper work, and he said, "Well, go to this medium. I know a woman in Ängelholm who told me things ten years ago that helped me a lot." The older I get, the stranger this story seems.

ARAM: This is when?

TOMMIE: This is January 1986. Sven gave me the name of this medium, Majken Ohlsson. She's just an ordinary lady, like a waitress in a cafeteria. "Why should I call her?" I asked. I don't

Photo: Eje Sjolander

Majken Olsson, October 1981

believe in that sort of thing, but Sven insisted I call. Years before, Sven had mentioned Swedenborg to me. There's something quite out of the ordinary in him. After some hesitation, I called her. She said, "You can come on Monday if you want—no, you can't, that's your birthday, isn't it?"

And it was!

"You'd better wait until Thursday."

"Is there anything I need to do to prepare?" I asked.

"Well, you can bring photos. I can tell you about the people in them."

So I brought photos of my daughter, Victoria, who was three months old, my grandmother, Delius, maybe Helen, and Bo Strömberg.

I drove down there—oh, it was really dreadful; it was pouring with rain as I drove. I was dead scared. I opened the door to her house, and she gasped like she'd seen a ghost. And I thought I'm in for it now. I'll probably die on the way back, and she's foreseen it. We went upstairs. She said, "I'll just put the potatoes on. My husband will come for lunch." She did that and then looked at me, staring, inspecting. "Well," she said, "there is only music around you. I only hear music. I hear flutes, and I hear guitars, is it?" At that time, I was writing *Notturno*. I was, at this time, completely unknown, perhaps a bit in the guitar world, but anyway, I started by showing her a photo of my grandmother, who had died a year and a half before. She looked at the photo and said, "Oh, thank God! She was the one who had cancer in the liver. It wasn't you. Because they said cancer of the liver when you came into the room." My grandmother died of cancer of the liver. What a thing to say! Then she said, "You have a blonde wife with a good singing voice who plays the piano." But Helen couldn't sing, she wasn't blonde, and she didn't play the piano or anything.

Then, the serious thing happened. She said, "Well, you're supposed to be great in some aspect of music, and it has to do with atmosphere." I couldn't grasp what she meant. She said, "There's a man sitting next to you in a wheelchair, and you're supposed to fulfill something he didn't complete." I showed her a photo of Delius. "He's English," she said, "but he lives in France. And, you know, he wasn't kind all the time. He has a child with a girl in America,[11] and he has some connection with a Roman bishop or something. He's helping you. He's sitting next to you. They will play your music for hundreds of years." I was completely stunned. From where came this information? She said, "The spirits are with you. Don't be afraid. You're under the protection of the White Eagle. There is another one helping you or within you."

"Who?"

"Victoria, a composer named Victoria." I didn't know any composer by that name. "He was brought up in Spain by monks," she said. "He wrote music for the Pope and lived at this address. Write this down," she said, "San Girolamo della Carità. And he, Victoria, has a connection with him," she said, pointing to Delius. "In the spiritual world, they are together." Interesting, since Delius wasn't religious at all.

We talked a bit more, and she went on. When I was to leave, she said a very strange thing to me. She said, "Do you know that Olof Palme will be elevated to a higher sphere? Very soon." One month later, he was shot dead in Stockholm. She didn't charge me any money. The drive home was scary. It was raining. My thoughts were racing. My whole system was undergoing a revolution. My whole world was turned upside down. I went immediately to Sven, took up a music dictionary, and looked for Victoria. Of course, he was there. But that wasn't enough—I've got to hear the music! So, Sven said, "Let's go down to Malmö to the conservatory there. We'll go to the library. They'll have some." So, he drove me down

---

11 See Tasmin Little's documentary film, *The Lost Child.*

there. When I went into that library, I didn't look, I went straight from intuition and pulled a record out. It was Benjamin Britten's *Prelude and Fugue on a Theme of Vittoria*![12] Sven stood next to me. And then, we went into a listening room and read about Victoria. You know, these old LP sleeves have a lot of text on the back. And I found that address the medium had mentioned! She couldn't have made that up! After that, I continued to study Delius and listened to a lot of Victoria. But then, I listened to Delius with other ears. I listened a lot to Beecham's recordings of *North County Sketches* and *Arabesque*, and it seemed less haunting and more profound. Delius became, to me, a mystic.

ARAM: . . . who was trying very hard to be a materialist?

TOMMIE: Sometimes I think he was actually praying while composing—the same sort of concentration you use when you're praying. Fenby used to say something similar.

ARAM: Same with you, perhaps.

TOMMIE: Yes, that's what I learned from that experience. What happened next was that I phoned an editor at a magazine called *Kvällsposten*, the editor for the cultural page, and I talked very enthusiastically about Delius. I wanted to spread Delius. I didn't care about what I was doing. It was Delius I wanted them to hear about. "Well," he said, "since you're so enthusiastic, why don't you write an article? If I like it, we'll take it. By the way, why don't you call Fenby? I've got his number." It was an unlisted number.

ARAM: He gave you Fenby's telephone number?

12 Vittoria is an alternate spelling of Victoria.

TOMMIE: Yes! So, I thought, well, I've got to call Fenby. He had recorded his *Songs of Farewell* with the London Royal Philharmonic and would record *Song of the High Hills* a few weeks later. I didn't know that then. So, I called him. The first thing I said was that I was calling from Sweden. He said, "Good Lord, you're calling from Sweden?" I said I was trying to compose and that I loved Delius' music so much, and he must have heard that I had a heart behind my words. "Well," he said, "will you be in England at some point?"

"Yes," I said, "I'm going within the month."

"Well," he said, "why don't you come see me then, and I'll take you out to lunch at the Royal Festival Hall or somewhere." So, I went there and saw this little man—he walked like Charlie Chaplin—and for an hour he talked only about this Swedish girl he was secretly engaged to when he lived with Delius—how much he loved her, her eyes were so beautiful, love of his life, and so on. It didn't work out. She was a Swedenborgian, and the family had been for generations. So, then Swedenborg turns up again. Fenby had visited her in Sweden but couldn't cope with the family and so on. She was from an upper-class family, and he was just a Yorkshire lad, self-taught.

Anyway, I had this lovely meeting with Fenby. I didn't talk about myself as a composer then. I wouldn't have dared. But I did ask him a lot of things about Delius, and then, he just turned pale, deathly pale, and started shaking. I didn't know what was happening. It was a panic attack. I asked, "What is it?" "Oh," he said, "it's the years with Delius. Sometimes, when I talk about those times, it just comes over me. I'll never get rid of it." While we were at the restaurant, a student of his from the Royal Academy came to say hello, and Fenby told him he was a hopeless composer and shouldn't be studying there, the music he'd been writing was nonsense, and so on. So, I thought, wow, this is not someone to trifle with.

ARAM: I won't ask you to elaborate too much on that.

TOMMIE: I asked Fenby, "Why did you burn all your work?" I knew he had composed a great amount of it and then destroyed it all. "Well, my boy," he said, "during my time with Delius, I realized that only genius matters in composition. And I didn't consider my work as being of genius." He didn't destroy all of it. He later sent me some church music he'd written, and I know he composed the score for *Jamaica Inn*.

ARAM: Alfred Hitchcock's *Jamaica Inn*?

TOMMIE: Yes, Fenby was on the way to Hollywood to write more music for Hitchcock, but the war intervened. Hitchcock was a great Delius fan. He actually used one of his pieces in a film.

ARAM: Which one?

TOMMIE: There's a guy, as usual, being chased, misunderstood, and he meets a blind man in the forest. And this blind man plays Delius on the piano.

ARAM: That sounds like *Saboteur*. In any case, did you stay in touch with Fenby often?

TOMMIE: Yes, and when I got back to Sweden three weeks later, I had a phone call from a lady speaking in broken Swedish. At that time, we were still preparing to do this play about Delius and wanted Fenby to help with it. We spent years on it. Anyway, the woman on the phone was named Soldanella Oyler. It was she to whom Fenby had been engaged. She said, "After fifty years, Eric Fenby has written to me and said, 'You have to talk to this

Swedish boy I just met.'" So, she started explaining who she was, her ancestry, that she'd been to Delius' house several times, and that she knew Mrs. Delius very well. She'd met Vaughan Williams, Hugo Alfven, and Verner von Heidenstam. She was directly related to Per Frigel, who arranged the Musikaliska Akademien[13] for King Gustaf III in the 1700s. He was a friend of Haydn's and Beethoven's and Cherubini's. Her uncle was the publisher of Strindberg's *A Blue Book* volumes and so on. I found myself entering a completely different world. We talked for hours, several times a week, for hours and hours. I would have proposed to her had she been my age. I really loved her like someone in my family. She was like something out of the 1700s. Later, she said she had two musical men in her life, Fenby and me.

ARAM: This was 1986, right? How old was Soldanella at the time?

TOMMIE: She was born in 1913, so perhaps seventy-three? Months later, I told her the story about the medium, and when I came to Victoria, she gasped. I said, "What is it?" "I'm just now holding 78 rpm discs with music of Victoria that Eric Fenby gave me in Grez-sur-Loing," she said. He used to play Victoria's music. He loved it so much. Then she said, "You shouldn't go to mediums when you're feeling insecure. And what you should do instead is read Swedenborg. You have to understand that you have all the answers within you. You don't need to go to a medium. You don't know what kind of spirit is talking through them. This time, you were lucky." I followed that advice. When I talked to Fenby on the

---

13 The Musikaliska Akidemien is the Royal Swedish Academy of Music.

Photo: Helen Haglund

Left to Right: Soldanella Oyler, Guido Vecchi, Tommie Haglund, Sven-Eric Johanson, ca. 1989.

phone once again, I asked him, "Why did you become a Catholic? You were born a Methodist." "Well," he said, "it was mostly the music of Victoria."

ARAM: How did Soldanella's interest in Swedenborg influence your own?

TOMMIE: When Soldanella told me to read Swedenborg, I felt a great relief that I could connect Christianity to this experience with the medium and that we have so little knowledge about what's really going on outside ourselves. Ironically, Swedenborg himself advises not to contact mediums, and yet that was the gateway to Swedenborg and the rest of my life. I had always looked with strong suspicion on people who spoke to mediums because these mediums are using gullible people to make money. And yet, if Majken Ohlsson was employing guesswork, it was extremely good, I guess. I think you have to be fanatically devoted to a cynical form of rationalism to explain that as guesswork only. I was brought up in a secular country with a state religion. We read the Bible in school and all that, and as a young boy, I had a strong attraction to religion. Coming into the Swedenborgian church in Stockholm, there is a painting of the sun over the altar, not a crucifix. I still don't understand the crucifixion. It seemed unbelievably cruel.

ARAM: Will you ever visit a medium again?

TOMMIE: No, never. And if someone proved to me that she was a phony, I'd believe it, but I'm still left with these things she said. These are difficult things to put into words—so many layers. Some scientists are convinced we're holograms. It's much easier for me to understand what is hidden through composition and put my thoughts about them into music. The writings of Swedenborg are, to me, about much more than community and social boundaries.

When Soldanella said, "If you believe in a spiritual world, avoid anything that has to do with mediums and read Swedenborg instead," that really made me come into balance. I read an interesting interview with Brahms where he's talking about Swedenborg giving him solace when he's worried. It was an American guy interviewing him in the 1890s, maybe. Another time, the same interviewer spoke with Strauss, and Strauss also talked about Swedenborg—a lot. The odd thing is, I can't find any music in the words—in Swedenborg's words.

ARAM: Maybe here and there.

TOMMIE: Before I met Soldanella in the 1980s, I heard a fine work by Arne Mellnäs called *Nocturne*. It's for soprano and chamber ensemble. The text has both Swedenborg and Blake in it. It was actually before I met Soldanella that I read about these visions of snakes crawling in hell, stenches, and all that sort of thing. At that time, I thought of Swedenborg's descriptions of heaven and hell as fantasies, really. In another of his books, he says that life without love is but flying feathers, *ulltappar*, and dung.[14] I would never have believed that Swedenborg would become so important to me. When I was listening to *Nocturne*, he was just a visionary, almost like Blake. But when I was properly introduced, his work became very important as a way to formulate these mystical experiences.

ARAM: To systematize the experiences?

TOMMIE: Yes. I look to Swedenborg for answers. I have so many questions, and I can live with that in music. But some things in Swedenborg are very hard to understand. I comprehend these mysteries by composing instead of sitting, reading chapter after chapter.

---

14 Haglund is referring here to *The Worship and Love of God* §85, which says something similar. The Swedish word *ulltappar* does not have an adequate English translation, but it roughly means "rolled up balls of wool fluff."

7: SOLDANELLA

ARAM: Did Soldanella know your family?

TOMMIE: Yes. Soldanella saw Helen quite often and my daughters and my parents. She was the godmother of my youngest daughter, Amanda. Soldanella never demanded attention and was always interesting to talk to. She had so much dry humor. Even when I made silly jokes, Soldanella kept listening carefully to everything.

ARAM: Soldanella really hovers in the music. Do you use her as a critical eye and ear?

TOMMIE: She does. Everywhere. Yes, an inner ear.

ARAM: So, coming back to this crucial question: what happened between *Notturno* and *Intensio Animi*? There was a significant transformation between these pieces. Your visit to the medium opened your eyes in a certain way, and Soldanella introducing you to Swedenborg is also important. But there must have been something else.

TOMMIE: You know, there was. I was sitting at Studiefrämjandet one night alone, and a chord came to me: C-C#-E-F-B-C-E♭-E.

I used that chord to build *Intensio Animi*. It just turned up in my head like a flash. I went home and tried it on the piano and found a whole new sense of tonality from that single chord. Everything I was aiming at came to me in that moment. It was like listening to eternity.

So, later, when I was composing *Intensio Animi*, I wanted to try it out on the piano. We had small kids, so I went to the theater at the park here in Halmstad, where there was a studio and a piano. I went there at night—I had a key. Anyway, I went there and came up with what I thought were very nice sections. But who can I ask? Soldanella, of course. "What do you think of this?" It was eleven in the evening, and I phoned her and played it through. "Play it again," she said. I played it a second time. "One more time," she said.

ARAM: There was a phone by the piano?

TOMMIE: Yes, I just put the phone up on the piano while I played. She said, "Write it down and send it to me so I can try it out on the piano myself." So, she did and commented that certain sections were like looking into crystal balls.

ARAM: What did Soldanella represent?

TOMMIE: Elegance, refinement, enormous curiosity, and a way of enjoying beauty. And a precious form of love you can't put your hands on physically. Her mother, Elsa Giöbel, was a Swedish painter and friend of Carl Larsson's, and the house was full of her paintings. She stopped painting when the modernists took over. Soldanella told me her father, Philip Oyler, burnt some of her mother's canvases—he didn't think women should paint. She was a close friend of Fanny Falkner—Strindberg's last love, a famous miniature painter—and she owned small portraits of the Danish king and queen Falkner had made in the first half of the twentieth century. "Ethereal" is a word I would use in describing Soldanella. It's around you all the time. I can feel her presence very often. I am talking to her in my mind. I think she would have loved this music I'm doing now. I miss her almost every day.

ARAM: I see you keep some memorabilia of your time with Soldanella.

TOMMIE: Yes, I've got her hat. She forgot it one time, and I kept it on the shelf. It'll always be there. And I have paintings from her mother, letters between her and Eric Fenby, and her copy of Fenby's book about Delius, with Fenby's dedication to her.

ARAM: That neighbor girl in the Ken Russel film about Delius—that's not supposed to be Soldanella, is it?

TOMMIE: It is, yes.

ARAM: But she wasn't like that.

TOMMIE: Not at all. It's not her at all, not a single bit of her. We watched the film together a few times, and she would always say, "I don't remember that conversation." But it was supposed to be her, yes.

ARAM: Delius says to Fenby in the film, "What are your intentions toward this girl? Marriage? She'll bring a fine dowry, not to sneer at, I admit. Go and amuse yourself with as many women as you can, but never marry. An artist should never marry, and if you have to marry, marry a girl who's more in love with your art than you." What was Soldanella doing in France? Was she there because her father was managing Theodore Pitcairn's[15] estate?

15 Theodore Pitcairn (1893–1973) was an American Swedenborgian

TOMMIE: Yes. Her parents had just divorced—something very unusual in those days. Philip Oyler moved to Dordogne, while Elsa stayed in Nora, where her family owned a peat factory. Soldanella was in Grez to visit her father, but they had very bad relations. For a while, her father wanted to disinherit her, though he was very positive about her engagement to Fenby.

ARAM: It seems Soldanella has a continuing role in your life.

TOMMIE: She was a window to a secret world. She could also be very demanding, you know. If she wanted to show you a thing, and you were tired, she'd say, "Well, look at this now." I did love her a great deal. We understood each other so deeply. And the humor she had—she was this upper-class woman to whom you could say the most bizarre things, and you'd wonder, how will she react now? Once, there was a Schnittke-Beethoven-Haglund festival in Denmark, and she was there. I was quite nervous. I had listened to the rehearsals; they were very good. People were sitting, waiting for the musicians. Soldanella was sitting next to me, and I suddenly had this feeling—I don't know what came over me. I said to her, "What would you think if I could just have a small bell and stand in front of the audience ringing it and saying, 'gooooooooodnight-a-ding-ding-ding-ding-ding, gooooooooodnight-a-ding-ding-ding-ding-ding,' like a Python sketch?" "Oh," she said, "it would be most embarrassing." [*Laughs.*] Nothing more than that, totally dry. Oh, there were so many things like that with her. I used to play Monty

---

theologian, renowned art collector, and author of numerous sermons and theological texts expounding the beliefs of the Lord's New Church which is Nova Hierosolyma.

Python sketches when she was bored, and she'd say, "Do you have another one?"

ARAM: Tell me about this print on the wall in the corner.

TOMMIE: I was about to write *Intensio Animi,* and for some reason, I was in Stockholm with my friend Stefan Petzén. We went to the Strindberg Museum where I saw a costume poster for one of his plays, *Svarte fanor*. A woman goes out of the picture, suffering. The face reminded me of Soldanella when she was younger. It was impossible to let go of the picture. When I got home, I phoned the Strindberg Museum, but they didn't have a poster of it for sale. They suggested I phone the artist, Charles Koroly, and I did.

ARAM: So that's a unique print. No one else has that.

TOMMIE: It's a vital picture, really. It's important. It's all there. When I phoned the artist, he asked me why I wanted the print. I said I was composing a piece for the Swedenborg Jubilee. He was silent for a while. Then, he erupted, "*För helvete*! Say that again!" "Swedenborg," I said. "*För helvete,*" he repeated. "I thought of Swedenborg while doing this picture. You'll have it," he said. "I'll send it immediately."

ARAM: There are clearly some things at work in your music that feel like resonance from Swedenborg and his books. Not in a direct or doctrinaire way. I'm not sure I want to say that to completely appreciate your music you have to also appreciate this man and his books, but maybe to fully understand it?

TOMMIE: I wouldn't want it to be that way, no.

ARAM: Do you think you have to come to the books as theology, per se, to see the connections?

Photo: Bo Stromberg

Costume poster from Strindberg's *Svarta fanor* by Charles Koroly.

TOMMIE: No, not for a second. You know, the Filarmónica de Bogotá's musicologist Alexander Casas Castro, who writes program notes for them, said similar things about my music in connection with a performance of *Serenata per Diotima* last year: you have to know something about Swedenborg to fully understand what I'm doing.

ARAM: What does that mean to you?

TOMMIE: [*Pause.*] It's up to you how you want to perceive the music.

ARAM: Well, that goes without saying, right? But why not another mystic or spiritual thinker? Why Swedenborg?

TOMMIE: I was twenty-seven when Soldanella introduced me to Swedenborg, and I felt, this is it. This explains so much to me—that we only know a fraction of what is hidden. I needed something: a church, a spiritual substance. But, under no circumstances do I want to be called a New Church artist—that would be too limiting. On the other hand, I certainly don't keep Swedenborg a secret.

ARAM: You don't advertise these ideas in the music, but they do emerge. I wonder how Soldanella's family came to know about it.

TOMMIE: I've wondered that, too.

ARAM: Soldanella's father, Philip Oyler, as you know, published a book called *The Generous Earth*. He is certainly an interesting figure: a member of the upper class but working for Theodore Pitcairn for years as an estate manager.

TOMMIE: His wife was upper class, absolutely. Soldanella, on her mother's side, came from an aristocratic family. Philip Oyler came from English nobility, a family known since 1066. Apart from that, he was related to Arthur Conan Doyle. I've got a book by Soldanella's cousin, about whom she had mixed feelings. She was a bit older than Soldanella. And she describes the Oyler family. Philip Oyler was a follower of Tolstoy—live off the land. He made

Soldanella's mother work with her hands, heavy work, more than she could do. And as I mentioned, he burned her paintings in the garden because, presumably, he thought women shouldn't paint. I have letters from Soldanella describing how evil he was sometimes. When Soldanella was to be born, he was certain it would be a boy. So, he called Soldanella "Soldaneil" until she was seven. They lived out in the English countryside, and just before Soldanella was to be born, they moved to Glastonbury in order to be in the realm of the Knights of the Round Table to give birth to her there.

ARAM: That's interesting. And yes, that book, *The Generous Earth*, really is Tolstoian, and that makes sense both in terms of the agrarian utopia Philip Oyler dreamed of and the idea that you build your own eternity within you. Tolstoy gave his book about utopia the title *The Kingdom of God Is Within You* for more than one reason.

TOMMIE: Yes, in many ways, I thought that what he was saying was that we build our own paradise within ourselves.

ARAM: Did you meet Philip Oyler?

TOMMIE: No, he died in 1973, and Soldanella's mother died in 1979, so I met neither of them. There was a Swedish television documentary about Soldanella's mother, *Den Brutna Liljan* [The Broken Lily].

ARAM: So, you were there for Soldanella's reunion with Fenby. When was that?

TOMMIE: Yes, John Ehde and I took Soldanella to England to see Fenby in May of 1988—for the first time in fifty-two years! I had just finished *Intensio Animi* for the Swedenborg Jubilee. I asked Fenby whether he'd care to take a look at my work. I wasn't sure if it was any good. "Yes," he said he would do that. But he was so exceptionally critical about his own and other people's work that I was really tense about what he'd say. Remember, he'd burned most of his own work. When I handed him my scores, I kept hearing his words about only genius mattering in composition. But I had to find out whether my work had any artistic value. So, I thought, well, if he says this is not good enough, then I'll just give up.

ARAM: How did Fenby and Soldanella treat each other after so long?

TOMMIE: Fenby had his wife, Rowena, with him. While John Ehde and I were having a lesson with Fenby at his studio in Piccadilly Circus somewhere, Soldanella and Rowena took a walk in Hyde Park. When we had all reassembled for afternoon tea at the Ritz, Fenby said to Soldanella, "Do you remember that old couple that used to come to Delius on Sundays? The ones who used to go to Johannes Brahms' home in Vienna for tea?"

ARAM: That's the first thing they said to each other after fifty-two years?

TOMMIE: Yes, as I remember it. But after that, they began invoking memories about Delius and Grez-sur-Loing. Later, I asked Soldanella, "Are you still in love with Fenby?" She said, "No, no, no. It came to nothing! I had to take care of my sick mother with typhoid." I have a letter written by Fenby to Soldanella in which he says he's disappointed that she gave him up—written the day after Delius died. I mentioned earlier that Fenby had even traveled to Sweden, I think, in 1935, to meet Soldanella and her mother. He met also with the Björck family, Strindberg's publishers, who were

Photo: Unknown

Eric Fenby, 1933

also Swedenborgians. Fenby himself was considering a conversion to Swedenborgianism. Soldanella's uncle was Albert Björck.[16]

Anyway, when Fenby and Soldanella met they were very friendly, very cordial, very English. But I think Soldanella did it for my sake more than for her own. She had already closed the door. So, when I wrote the string quartet just after Soldanella died, I dedicated it to her. At one point, in the ending, I ask where she is in the sound of the notes, C-A♭-G: *where-are-you?*

---

16 Albert Björck (1857–1938) was a Swedish pastor, publisher of Strindberg's *A Blue Book* volumes, and author of several books and pamphlets about Swedenborgianism, including *The Hague Position* and *Emanuel Swedenborgs betydelse för framtiden*.

ARAM: They never saw each other again?

TOMMIE: They never saw each other again—probably wrote Christmas cards. Roger Fenby, Eric's son, visited me twice some years after Eric died. He wrote me a letter saying he'd heard some of my music, and so on, that he used to mention me, and that he'd discovered 150 letters written by Eric to his mother from Grez-sur-Loing in the 1930s. Much of the context of those letters is Soldanella, saying she was the love of his life. Roger discovered them in the attic. He didn't even know about Soldanella. So, he wanted to find out what I knew and get to know this woman that his father had loved so much.

8: SWEDENBORG

ARAM: So, you returned to Halmstad after London and waited for Fenby to phone you about your composition.

TOMMIE: Yes, I went home and waited anxiously every day for him to call—with a mixture of fear and hope. He said, "I'll call you in two weeks and tell you exactly what I think." Two weeks went by, three weeks. Then the phone rang, and Helen said, "It's Eric Fenby."

ARAM: You're thinking the rest of your life would change by this one phone call.

TOMMIE: Yes, and he's waited three weeks, and now, he's finally thinking he has to say something. Or his wife has said, you *must* call. That's what I was thinking. But he said, "My dear boy! This is what you should do! You can call me. You can send me things!" After that, I had long talks with him about everything. In fact, for the last recording he was going to make for the Royal Philharmonic, he phoned me and asked what pieces by Delius he should conduct. I told him the story about the medium, and he wasn't surprised.

ARAM: So, it's 1988. You're twenty-nine years old, and you've put the guitar on the shelf. You, Helen, Victoria, and Amanda have moved to a 150-year-old house in the countryside outside Harplinge. And it was also at this time you began reading Swedenborg.

TOMMIE: Yes. There was a rumor that the house was haunted. I once saw an old woman walking in the house. A few hundred meters away, there was a count whose caretakers lived there. There was a basement—just a plain cellar with nothing in it. Beside the stairs, there was a fridge and a bottle crate. One evening, when I was sitting, composing, I heard a bang. So, I opened the door, and one of the bottles was upside down, standing on its nose. Strange? Then, when we moved out of the house years later, there was a flood in the basement. When the water was gone, I walked down, and there was a bottle on its nose.

Soldanella came to visit very often. Once, she asked me to play something by Dowland. And as she sat there listening, she said, "Hello, Helen." But there was no one there. She said there was someone there, holding her shoulder very hard. She thought it was Helen. But there was no one. And at night—when you have these old doors, they're stuck shut, and yet sometimes they would just open. But it was never unpleasant—just someone wandering around.

ARAM: Let's turn back in time a little bit and talk more about the process of composing *Intensio Animi*.

TOMMIE: There was this Jubilee coming up, the 300th anniversary of Swedenborg's birth, in 1988. I worked feverishly on

Intensio Animi for the Swedenborg Society in Stockholm. It was my first commission—I wonder if Soldanella wasn't behind that. I didn't know how it would turn out. I thought I might base it on Swedenborg's *Dream Diary*, so I re-read it and tried to get into that mental state.

Anyway, I was working on *Intensio Animi* and was in such a state of mind, exploring parts of my brain that I had never before visited. The sky was opening. There was a new world. I wanted to write from my own perspective, from all these scores I had been studying. When I'd finished *Intensio Animi*, John Ehde took it to a pianist in Copenhagen. They played it in Vienna, in the Hochschule für Musik. The cellist there, who was with the Vienna Philharmonic, recommended that it be played in a concert. So, they did that as a kind of hidden first premiere of the piece, to see what it was like. It came out fine. Then, we took it to Stockholm for the Swedenborg Jubilee. I had no idea that the press would come. The big press, Scandinavia's largest newspapers, came with their best music critics. They were there, and yet I hardly felt like a composer. They'd written about me before, here in Halmstad, but this was Stockholm. They played Beethoven, Delius, Sæverud, and *Intensio Animi*. Soldanella was there. Karin Swedenborg was there. They were all there. When the concert was over, as I was thanking the musicians, I looked around and a line of people was standing there, some of them in tears, to thank me. I was utterly surprised. I got back to Halmstad and didn't think more about it, and someone called from the local radio station and said, "Have you seen the reviews?"

"What reviews?"

"In Stockholm."

"About what?"

"About your music, of course!" I didn't subscribe to those newspapers. So, Stefan Petzén, a good friend who writes tunes and songs, went with me to the petrol station nearby, and we bought the papers and read the reviews, and I just couldn't believe what they were saying! It was a ravishing thing that opened so many doors for me. And then suddenly, I was on television with Håkan Hagegård[17] and Nicolai Gedda[18] as a representative of the "new music."

ARAM: I take it you never went back and saw the medium?

TOMMIE: [*Pause.*] I did, with Soldanella. You know what she did? She came here once carrying that bust of Mozart that's on the grand piano as a present. One of my friends told me Majken, the medium, was here in town, so we decided to invite her here along with some other people. So Majken came to my house—not this one, the haunted one. The next day, Soldanella said, "Maybe we should go and see her. Do you want to go see her? Just you and I go."

I said, "Yes, I think I do." I didn't remind her she had told me not to. You see, Majken and Soldanella didn't speak when they were together in the house. There were so many people there they didn't get a chance to speak to each other. I think that's why Soldanella wanted to see her. So, we drove down to Ängelholm, and the medium immediately started talking about Soldanella's father—describing him, clothing, habits, and so on. Everything

17 Håkan Hagegård (1945–) is a Swedish baritone who has appeared on numerous records, as well as in operas and films, including Bergman's *The Magic Flute.*

18 Nicolai Gedda (1925–2017) was a celebrated Swedish tenor who made hundreds of recordings and starred in as many operas.

Photo: Tommie Haglund

Karin Swedenborg with Tommie's daughters, Amanda and Victoria, and Helen Haglund, ca. 1990

fit. Then she said, "Well, you don't need to worry about cancer or any other diseases."

Then, a strange thing happened. It wasn't a long meeting, and as we were about to go, the medium said to Soldanella, "Someone's been digging a big hole next to your house." Soldanella protested that there had never been one. She'd never heard of anything like that. They went on arguing. Neither of us could understand why the medium was saying it. She was so persistent about it. So Soldanella went home and phoned me and said, "Do you know what I've seen? They've dug a big hole in the neighbors' garden with a machine."

9: SVEN-ERIC

ARAM: You learned from many different people. How did you meet Sven-Eric Johanson?

TOMMIE: There was a cellist named Guido Vecchi, who was considered to be the foremost Swedish cellist of his generation—which would have been the 1950s–60s. He would sit on the juries for town orchestras to decide which musicians would be hired. He admired my music and supported me so much. He was in his late seventies when we met. He was the first cellist in the Gothenburg Symphony Orchestra. I think he was born in 1910. He used to come here because there was a regional orchestra, and he was the censor for Musik i Halland.[19]

Anyway, in 1989, he'd heard about *Intensio Animi*, so he looked me up and found me and wondered if he could visit. He came for

19 Musik i Halland was a state-financed organization promoting musical appreciation in the Halland region. At the time, they had their own wind quintet and string quintet, the members of which were employees of the state. Vecchi's job was to decide who could be hired as members of these quintets.

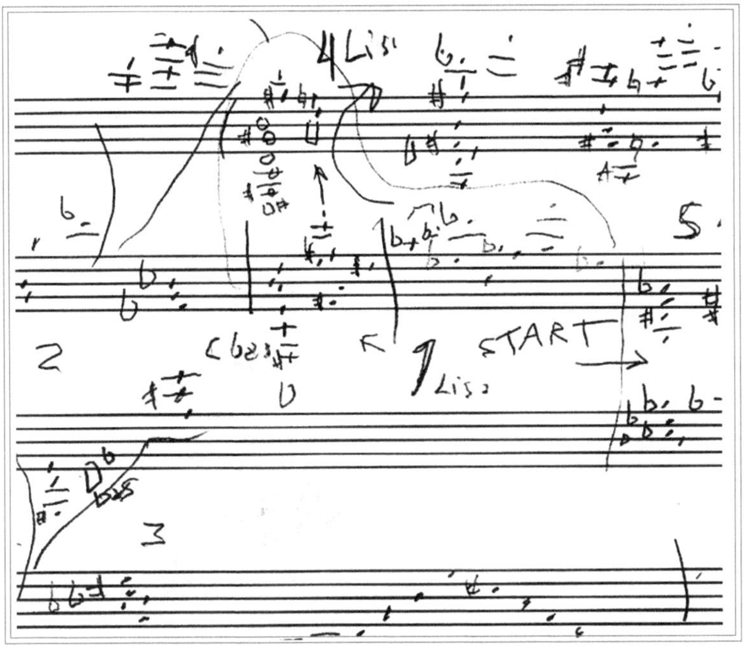

A portion of a hand-written *Symphony* score example by Tommie Haglund.

dinner and told us about this fantastic life. He had met Shostakovich, Strauss, Grieg's wife, everyone. He loved *Intensio Animi*. He wanted to hear it again and again. After that, he followed everything I did, and I could ask him for help. He was full of jokes! He told Sven-Eric Johanson, a famous Gothenburg composer, about me. So, when Sven-Eric was to have an organ concert here in Halmstad, he called me up to see if we could meet based on Guido's recommendation. I thought, now this is a real composer coming to see me—a real composer, a legend!

This was, I think, 1989. When he arrived in Halmstad, he phoned and asked if I could pick him up at the station. So, I did, and I drove

Sven-Eric Johanson, ca. early 1990s

him out to where Helen and I were living. Sven-Eric, I remember, wore a red sports jacket and was dressed like a teenager. He was seventy or so at that time. We listened to *Intensio Animi,* and he said he really liked it. When I drove him to his organ concert, I very gently asked whether I could have some lessons with him if he had the time. I had never had composition lessons, apart from with Fenby. He replied, "Yes, if there is anything I can teach you. You can come for free anytime." This, of course, was him being overly modest. But he said, "You don't have to pay anything. Come whenever you want." That was the beginning of a relationship that went on until his death.

ARAM: Your time with Sven-Eric was formative, even if that's not so evident in the music. Most people outside Sweden won't know who he was.

TOMMIE: Oh, right. I knew about him for a long time. He was well known—still is. He was one of the major figures in Swedish musical life from the '40s to the '90s. The Monday Group's influence on more traditional Swedish composers was highly destructive. This has nothing to do with Sven-Eric. He didn't like how badly these old composers were treated. Karl-Birger Blomdahl, who was the chief of Swedish Radio—classical music radio—almost forced a kind of experimentalism on everyone. He excluded everyone who was not atonal or modernist, not part of that movement, like Lars-Erik Larsson, Erland von Koch, and Dag Wiren—composers who kept the tonal tradition.

Lars-Erik Larsson was studying with Alban Berg in Vienna in the '30s. He lived in Helsingborg, and I got to know him a bit at the end of his life. We had a couple of—for me—interesting talks before he died. He is one of the more celebrated Swedish composers, but he wrote tonal music, perhaps close to Bartok. Sometimes, to my ears a bit dry and woody, sometimes with great romantic beauty, but well loved. The Monday Group considered him an enemy because he wrote too much tonal music. He wrote music that people loved listening to. In a way, you could consider him a *folkhem*[20] composer, but that's just my take. The reason I got

20 *Folkhem* is a Swedish term that translates to "people's home" and is used as a euphemism for a society based on welfare and social security, as well as the values of the Swedish welfare state.

in touch with him was because Bo Strömberg and I wanted to ask him to write guitar pieces for our publishing company. I phoned him up, but he said he didn't write music any longer. Anyway, at that time, the followers of the Monday Group dominated institutions with their modernistic influence, and because of this, Larsson felt no one was interested in him. I didn't think this was true, and I encouraged him to start writing again. I told him I thought something new was on the way in the world of music. I sensed there was an undercurrent of musicians reacting against the sometimes atonal modernism. They lacked warmth, long phrasing, and melody. They were hostile to these things. I got to talking about how I also didn't want to write atonal music, and I didn't know where to turn because of the existing trends. I also asked him what it was like to study with Berg. And he said that Berg was an extremely kind man, a bit shy, who had his pupils study Bach and baroque counterpoint, very traditional exercises, despite the fact that Berg himself was a partly serialist composer.

Anyway, Sven-Eric was once a member of the Monday Group, but he was the black sheep, you see. He didn't marginalize anyone and, in fact, was a bit marginalized himself because he did things like compose a one-man opera with himself in the single role. Or take his cello concerto, which came to the middle point and then ran backward! So many spectacular things that people sometimes didn't take seriously, and yet he was the most serious composer I ever met. They couldn't put him in a box. Once, he wrote in the newspaper that he wanted to send himself up in a hot air balloon over Öland and conduct ten rock bands with a laser stick, a bit like something Stockhausen would do. But he was really serious and skilled and knew every musical style backwards and forwards, from the Middle Ages to twelve-tone.

ARAM: Why did Blomdahl exclude everything pre-war? He had control of radio programming?

TOMMIE: Perhaps it was part of the post-war attitude. In Social Democratic Sweden, modernism was regarded very well. People like Olof Palme and others before him in the government encouraged modernism and functionalist styles and stuff like that. Modernism was part of Swedish society at the time, but it was also very much of an elitist thing. The composers all adored Schönberg, of course, and, in a way, I did as well—not as a musical titan, but as an interesting person who was needed to eliminate all of traditional music's conventional elements, with dissonance predominating. That was only partly successful—after all, now we hear *Gurreliender* more often than we hear the twelve-tone music. Sometimes, I feel he was so expressive that he had to confine himself in this rigid system to contain himself. He was a master.

ARAM: Did you ever meet Blomdahl?

TOMMIE: No, he died in 1968, before I was composing. And I don't want to denigrate the whole legacy of the Monday Group. I think this was a phase we had to go through. Their legacy started to die in the '80s and collapsed, I think, at the same time the wall came down in Berlin. The whole concept collapsed. Other kinds of music turned up.

ARAM: So, Sven-Eric was involved with this group but not with this sort of modernist cartel?

TOMMIE: No, in fact, Sven-Eric moved from Stockholm to Gothenburg and established himself as a composer there. He was considered eccentric. He had the Dali mustache, big hair, uncombed, flying all over. Very kind, wild. I felt so safe with him. I felt immense support from him, and he treated me as a colleague, for which I was quite underprepared. He could be, as his wife said, a mythomaniac—the King of Myths—as she called him with a glimmer in her eye. You didn't know sometimes whether he was kidding you. In fact, in Gothenburg they had a city tram carriage named after him. He created a lot of happenings. But to me, he was a truly serious composer who sometimes wanted to confuse his audience.

ARAM: But he had few performances?

TOMMIE: Oh no, he did quite a lot. Nowadays, the ones that capture the public imagination are his choral works. I wouldn't say they're easy listening, but they are more accessible than some of the rest.

The first encounter I had with Sven-Eric was actually sometime in the beginning of the 1980s. I mentioned before I had this proposal from one of the Swedish newspapers to write this article on Delius. Sven-Eric used to lecture on his own life and bring Delius' *Requiem* around with him to play at the lectures as an example of something that had impacted him. He was a great fan of Delius despite the complete difference in style. Delius would have loathed most of Sven-Eric's music—would have totally dismissed it. I contacted Sven-Eric about this Delius article in 1985 or '86. I hadn't at that time begun to compose seriously, so I didn't want to introduce myself as a composer. What I wanted was a contemporary composer's comment on Delius' music for the newspaper article. We had a chat about Delius, nothing else. He had some very positive things to say about Delius; he thought his music had a future, there was something unique in it, and so on. Then, we didn't have any contact until 1989, when he was to come, as I said, to Halmstad for an organ concert, and Guido Vecchi set us up. I rarely heard him play any other music but his own, and he improvised a lot. He was a very good improviser. He was completely free. At the end of his life, he wanted me to have his grand piano. We didn't have space enough, and it was in lousy condition. We already had two grand pianos plus an upright. Anyway, that's beside the point.

A few months later, his wife called me and said she needed to go to a rest home for her nerves, so could Helen and I host Sven-Eric and the two children for a month in the summer. This was still 1989. And I'm thinking, this great composer is coming to stay with us! Well, he came! I remember we sat up many nights talking about Strauss. He played extracts, and we discussed everything—Scriabin, Liszt, his lessons with Otto Olsson, and when he played viola in an orchestra conducted by Hugo Alfven. He was to conduct one of his own symphonies, and when he was to do the third movement, he couldn't do it—he was a hopeless conductor, so he said, "I don't give a damn about the scherzo. Let's not do it!"

After a few days we had a phone call from a very upset wife saying he had overspent by two hundred thousand Swedish kroner.

ARAM: How did he do that?

TOMMIE: By kindness. The money was to pay taxes. For years, he hadn't paid any tax for his compositions. He had given it to his son-in-law, who tried to compose but didn't succeed. Sven-Eric was not a practical man. Just like me. But he was even more impractical than I am! His wife was always nervous and high-strung. He loved her immensely. He even had a Karin theme built into the structure of all of his compositions, which was for her. He was devastated about this tax debt, so he called his friend Stig Gustav—whose surname was actually Schönberg!—and told him what had happened, and Stig Gustav said—I overheard him. I sat next to him while he had this conversation—he said, "Why don't you phone the doctor and have yourself declared irresponsible?" And he did! He didn't care! He tried maybe fifty times to apply for a driver's license and finally gave up. So, he was declared irresponsible and managed to get the debt reduced to fifty thousand kroner and paid it off. But before he knew that, he instantly wanted to go to the *systembolaget* (alcohol store) and buy whiskey. The first lessons we had were really whiskey and John Wayne films. He just wanted to escape.

But it calmed down. I had this commission. There was to be an international music festival at the time Sven-Eric lived with us. I had a commission from Guido Vecchi to write for eight cellos. One of the cellists, Torleif Thedéen, had recorded often for BIS Records as a soloist. He turned ill, so the concert was canceled. Guido then called me and said, "Can't you write something for cello?" I said, "But I have Sven-Eric living here." "Oh, then write something for him and me," he said. "You have two weeks!" So, I started to compose *Fiori*—the title was Sven-Eric's suggestion. Sven-Eric had one request: that I include serialistic stuff so he could go wild and improvise in the middle of the piece.

ARAM: Sven-Eric was still enamored of Schönberg at this stage?

TOMMIE: He admired him unconditionally. But at the same time, he was turning more and more towards romantic music. This is particularly noticeable in his final symphony, *Chez*

Nous, where he pours out nostalgic feeling without restraint in a way that baffled me. I listened to that symphony together with him, and when that romantic part came, he was shaking. He had a big heart, and I wonder if he hadn't wanted to write more music that was emotionally focused. Anyway, I started to compose *Fiori* and was slightly annoyed as he hung over my shoulder at work. So, I took the car and drove to Helen's office at the university and sat there till late at night. Every evening, he'd wait up until three a.m. on the couch to see what I'd written. It was touching in a way that he was so interested. What amazed me was that when we were to rehearse this on the organ, he took each single chord and held it, "Hmmmm, yes, yes." Took the next one, held it, "Hmmmm, ahh-ha, yes." Then, the next one, and the next one. I thought, isn't he going to play it through rhythmically?

ARAM: As if the spaces between the notes don't matter.

TOMMIE: Nothing! So, the concert began to get closer and closer, and he had written a Swedenborg symphony for organ. He called it a symphony, but it was an organ piece—mostly improvised. I've never seen any of it written down. He was to perform that. There was to be my piece for organ and cello, and they were to play some, as Bream would say, lollipops and meringues. So, three days before the concert, we couldn't get ahold of Guido Vecchi. We couldn't find him. We didn't even know if he'd received the music. I'd sent it but hadn't heard anything. We rang his neighbor, finally, and he said, "Well, no, Guido's gone to Lund, staying at his sister's flat." He gave us the address, but we couldn't get the phone number. So, Sven-Eric and I took my Volvo PV down there. He wanted to stop the car some place where Rilke used to live. We stayed there a time, and Sven-Eric read Rilke poems, and then we finally reached Lund and found this flat. It's in one of the nicer parts of the city where she lived. She wasn't there, but Guido was there. We took the music out and put it in front of him. Sven-Eric played the organ part on the piano. Guido played the cello. After that, they started dancing and shouting, "We have a premiere! We have a premiere!" Guido tore down a poster off the wall—a very beautiful poster—and wrote *VI HADE EN PREMIERE HÄR* (We had a premiere here) on the back! I wish I had that now!

ARAM: [*Laughs.*] His sister probably came home, found it, and threw it away.

TOMMIE: Yes, most likely. That stupid brother of mine—who was eighty! Anyway, at the premiere, the real premiere, I was so nervous because I'd never heard them really play it through. The press was there. They were going to write about the music. Sven-Eric was drinking. We had this case of strong beer in the sacristy. Guido had his jacket and tails and a bow tie on, and Sven-Eric was drinking beer in his tracksuit and white tube socks, no shoes, playing the organ. They played the piece, and he did a very eccentric thing with the serialist part. He was using half-registers on the organ, so it sounded like circus music. It turned out to be a great success, but the press wrote very badly about both his composition and him, which was very unfair. It was very unfair. But among people, he was sort of contaminated by this reputation of being the black sheep in the establishment. You never knew whether he was kidding or not, and the press can't manage that. And the tracksuit did not help present him as a serious composer, which he was. He was, really. I miss him so much.

ARAM: The contrast was too much for the critics.

TOMMIE: Yes, and I got very good reviews, thanks to Sven-Eric and Guido. Sven-Eric's symphony was better than everything else. *Fiori* was just a bagatelle, comparatively. Sven-Eric was furious about the reviews but glad for my sake. He was still living with us when they appeared. It was summertime, but he wanted to show us a place where, later, he would invite us every Christmas for dinner. We went to this hotel owned by Per Gessle from Roxette—I actually programmed the music for his wedding. So, we went out to this hotel on the beach. For some reason, we got into an empty restaurant. There was no one else there. It was a very posh place, but everyone was out swimming, I guess. Sven-Eric heard some music on the stereo. It was Stevie Wonder's "I Just Called to Say I Love You." "Oh my God," he shouts. "It's our tune!" His and Karin's. "When we were in Tunisia," he said, "we danced to this tune. I was wearing a white suit, and she, a red dress, and everyone stopped to look at us." So, I said, "Why don't you use the first few bars of that song in your symphony for the Helsingborg Symphony Orchestra?" And he did, and John Ehde played the opening phrase as a solo.

Anyway, the whole time he stayed with us I learned so much. He listened to my points of view very carefully. He said it was important to know what you want to express and learn how to master it. He really helped me with that. There weren't many lessons, but many discussions about the scores—how Victoria used mistakes on purpose to create effects. He knew everything about that.

So, the summer went by, and on Christmas Eve, he was in Halmstad again, calling me from the same hotel. "Tommie," he said, "have you got any mustache wax?" "No," I said, "I don't even have a mustache!" What happened was that he was to have dinner with someone important, and he'd been sitting in the sauna, so his Dali mustache had drooped. He couldn't get it back into position. "Have you tried toothpaste?" I asked. He said, "No, but I'll try." And he did. He phoned back. "It doesn't work!" So, I said, "My wife has got some hair gel, but can't you ask if they have something at the hotel?" "Well, they haven't!" he cried. So, I said, "OK, I'll come with it." So, I drove out there. Well, there he stood at this posh hotel by the reception in his bathing robe, with his mustache drooping down!

ARAM: What would you say you learned specifically during your time with him?

TOMMIE: Oh, we went through so much together. Hindemith's *Unterweisung im Tonsatz*,[21] Alois Hába's essentials of the quarter-tone system, Scriabin's "Le Poème du Feu," Delius' *Song of the High Hills*, lots of other scores, Alban Berg's *Voríšek*. We went through it all very carefully. He was very tuned into that stuff. I came to him with my second commission, the chamber piece *Voces*. I'd come up with the introduction and had written it out, and he said it was so bright, and that was very encouraging. Anyway, he was a fantastic inspiration, and I'm fortunate he really took to me. He even made a speech to the Royal Academy about me. He wrote letters of introduction for grants. He was so generous. All the clowning is just part of what is so nice to remember. It's important sometimes—it releases tension when you have to

---

21 Composer Paul Hindemith's book on music theory aimed primarily to restore a solid music foundation to composition amidst the modernist trend toward aleatory techniques and as an antidote to Schönberg's atonal twelve-tone system.

go in and be so serious. But Sven-Eric and I really bonded. Since he was so fond of Delius, and I was a student of Fenby's as well, I asked if he wanted to talk to Fenby. "Yes!" he said. So, we phoned from the school where I used to teach old ladies. I still had the key. During that conversation, Sven-Eric told Fenby he'd written an opera, a *Lord of the Rings* cycle. But the rights were bought up by Hollywood, and they stopped it.

ARAM: What a great shame. Reminds me of Jodorowsky's *Dune*. I wonder what happened to Sven-Eric's score.

TOMMIE: I don't know. No idea. I miss him a lot sometimes, really. When I hear his music, it's heartbreaking. Very early, he realized I wasn't going to go into the late Schönberg style, wasn't going to compose twelve-tone. He said, "You have your own way. Just keep to that." That's what he told me. So, I followed that. He came to some of the Swedenborgian services in Gothenburg, actually. I remember everyone there being very impressed by Sven-Eric's ability to lead the singing in the service.

ARAM: If Sven-Eric wrote a work based on Swedenborg for the festival, what inspired him to do so?

TOMMIE: I don't want to take the honor for that. He already knew about Swedenborg, as most educated people here do, but he hadn't yet gone into the books as in-depth as he did later on. He also wrote a Swedenborg string trio that was premiered in Stockholm at the House of Culture, a concert with his and my music together. That was recorded by Swedish radio as well. There are so many stories about him. It's endless. Could be its own book, funny stories about Sven-Eric. Guido Vecchi told me they had been part of an entertainment program on Swedish television in the 1960s. For some reason, they were given a live lobster, which they took with them on the tram in Gothenburg. They were both quite intoxicated and Sven-Eric ended up in Guido's summer house, while Guido went to Sven-Eric's apartment. In the morning Sven-Eric woke up, and the lobster was crawling around on the floor. He called his own home, and Guido answered. He asks Guido, "Where am I?" Guido answers, "You're with me." So, Sven-Eric says, "Then where are you?" And Guido answers, "Well, I'm with you!"

ARAM: [*Laughs.*] Have you dedicated anything to him?

TOMMIE: Yes, *Fiori* was dedicated to him and Guido Vecchi and Helen. Sven-Eric was also the one who suggested Gehrmans[22] consider publishing my music. He phoned, so they took me on.

ARAM: Is he still with you?

TOMMIE: Yes. When I compose, he's there. Quite often, when I finish a piece, I feel I want to take it to him, show it, and ask him what he thinks. I was too ill to visit him on his deathbed, and I regret that, but I did manage to attend the memorial. I hadn't played his music for many years until recently. I played his symphony, *Chez Nous,* and it stirred up tears.

22 Gehrmans Musikförlag is Haglund's music publisher.

10: ELISABET

Compositions: Meditation

ARAM: In 1990, you completed two versions of *Voces*, one for wind quintet and string quintet, and one for orchestra; a piano piece called *Meditation*; as well as the violin piece, *L'Infinito*. At the same time, your marriage was in epic turmoil, and you met Elisabet, your future wife. That's a lot for one year, and there's a sense it may have contributed to problems with your health.

TOMMIE: Not only all that, I was just starting to get a sense of being known, which brings with it a lot of stress. There was a lot of chaos, but it wasn't all terrible. I had a prize from one of the major newspapers here. They have a cultural prize, a large sum of money. The usual thing is that you do a performance. The poet reads his poem, that kind of thing. John Ehde, the cellist, used to do magic tricks. We knew a guy who had written eight thousand songs. He's a bit of a savant—he died recently. The rhymes are extremely naïve and absurd but fantastic all the same. Hans Jacobsson, or Hasse. Big fellow, big beard! We had him involved with the concert. And all these posh ladies came, the so-called establishment, to see Tommie Haglund, the composer, and John Ehde, the cellist, and we did a fine performance in the concert hall—at first. The concert started with me reading a poem by Ekelöf.[23] Very serious. And John played some Bach. Then suddenly, Hasse came in with a song, "Dance boogie-woogie with your mother, dance boogie-woogie with your father, dance boogie-woogie till you drop dead." And we had some girls whom we called Hasse's Harem, and they did some boogie-woogie dance. And there was one song about sausages as well. You can imagine the old ladies in the audience looking at this. And then I announced, very seriously, that we would have a premiere of a new piece by Tommie Haglund. Our first plan was to bring a lawnmower into the concert hall, but when we rehearsed with it, we determined the gas would poison everyone, so we had a food processor instead. I played the piano very seriously for a time, and at the climax, John switched on the food processor. We tried to match the pitch of the piano with the machine. Finally, John fell off the chair with the machine. The reviews the next day said, "Cellist knocked dead by musical inferno."

ARAM: [*Laughs.*] Where and when did you meet Elisabet?

TOMMIE: In the spring of 1990, Sven and I went to a talk she held at the ABF about a music project founded by Sheila Nelson, a violin teacher. It's a program called the Tower Hamlet String Project, which worked with children and families in London's East End. Sven took me to this talk, and when I saw and heard Elisabet,

---

23 Gunnar Ekelöf (1907–1968) was a Swedish poet and writer, often cited as Sweden's first surrealist poet.

I immediately felt she had something I couldn't describe clearly: a strong intellect, and she was very beautiful. Also, she had an energy that was both challenging and inspiring. Since we had lived in London at the same time, we got talking after her lecture. She moved from England with two daughters, Julia and Clara, who were almost the same age as my two girls, Victoria and Amanda. So, jumping forward two years to when I had just started a project with children and classical music—I wanted to teach them to listen and discover the nuances in classical music and to widen their imaginations. I had another partner for this, but two weeks before we were to start, she phoned and said she was adopting a baby from Brazil. They'd been waiting five years, she and her husband, and suddenly it was time. So she couldn't do these workshops with me. I thought, what am I going to do? This was to be part of my income! This woman suggested I ask Elisabet—and that's how we got together. This was solid luck. She loves my music!

ARAM: She does? [*Laughs.*]

TOMMIE: Yes, she does! And then—actually, a little while before I met Elisabet, I had a student who had studied guitar with me, Martin Andersson. I'd helped him get into a music college for classical guitar. He studied there for two years, returned to Halmstad, met a girl, got married, and she became pregnant. They came out to see Helen and me a few times; always joyful and full of humor, Martin was. Just after I met Elisabet, I had a phone call from the director of ABF, where Martin also worked, and he said, "Tommie, are you sitting down?" "No! Why?" "Well, please sit. Martin's just jumped out in front of a train." It was two weeks before his baby was to be born. I had a phone call from his wife, Anette, and she

Photo: Tommie Haglund, retouched by Bo Strömberg

Elisabet Löfberg Haglund, ca. 1995

said, "Tommie, Martin would really have liked it if you'd write something for his funeral." That was where *Meditation* came from. It's a short piece for piano, which later was transcribed for organ. But who was going to play it? Elisabet, of course. She studied it so thoroughly and played it so well. That's how she got attached to the music. She feels it, maybe in a way I don't, but also very much as I feel it, and that's how I fell in love with her, through the music.

I have learned so much from her, and she has the ability to calm me down. Also, she can handle me when I sometimes go into a state of being uncompromising. Apart from the fact that she's so beautiful, she is the ultimate love of my life. And she doesn't have to tell me how she feels about my work. I can feel it. She's very organized and makes sure I'm on schedule and is very protective. I couldn't dream of knowing someone more perfect. I can't organize my own life the way she can do it—and the household. Sometimes, I'm playing a passage of music, and she doesn't like it, but she's always right. She has a fine ear.

ARAM (Turning to ELISABET): Do you agree with this? [*Laughs.*] Why don't you put on record something about your background and how you see yourself in addition to helping manage Tommie's career.

ELISABET: I am a music teacher—piano, ensemble, for example—so to some extent I understand what Tommie does, what it involves. Not entirely, of course, but a fair amount. We also share a general big interest in music and music history, which I think is good for both of us. We can discuss and talk about these things and understand what we talk about. I think it would be difficult for Tommie to have a partner who had no interest or understanding about music.

My everyday life is obviously very different as I teach and meet lots of people every day to whom I must adjust myself, compromise with, and generally fit in with, whereas Tommie has nobody he has to take into consideration that way. This makes our situations very different. We have quite different tempi as well. I am always working fast, and he, slowly, so sometimes, we are a little out of phase. I have helped him quite a lot in writing the manuscripts on the computer and playing through what he has written if it's not too complex.

I must admit that my way of having a good overview of things probably has helped Tommie a lot since he is a bit disorganized when it comes to practical things like paying bills, booking tickets, finding stuff around the house that he has mislaid, and so on. He hates that sort of thing, and I hate waiting for him to get it done, so I mainly just deal with it.

ARAM: We've been talking mainly in this book about Tommie's life and development as a composer from his own point of view. How has it looked, from your own perspective, as he has made new, deeper inroads into himself through the music?

ELISABET: It's hard for me, or anybody, to answer that as nobody can see inside his mind. From my point of view, he has gone through some phases, but nevertheless, I think all the music is like one long, uninterrupted piece. They are sort of connected to each other, with some small difference from piece to piece.

When he was very ill, the music obviously reflected that. I had great difficulties with the violin concerto, for example. Couldn't listen to that at all when it was first completed. And after that terrible period, he couldn't compose at all for over a year. Or rather, he decided not to. He wanted to have some space, I think. And when he started again, he felt he couldn't get into these dark and harrowing places like the violin concerto again. He had to do different things.

When it comes to what he listens to, he has these periods. When the girls still lived at home, we had a year and a half of Dowland, the same amount of time of Schumann, then Rameau, and so on. So, we all got infused by a certain composer for quite a long time!

ARAM: Which of Tommie's works do you have the most special or personal resonance with and why?

ELISABET: *Miraggio* and *La Rosa Profunda,* partly because they are written for me but, of course, also for the quality of the music.

I think it is hard to describe the emotions music stirs up within. It can sound too banal. But those two pieces give me a feeling of a strange mixture of joy, deep sadness, peace, and eternity.

Sollievo is also a favorite. It came about after Tommie had been very ill and in an almost constant state of anxiety. And this piece is really *sollievo,* and I love the link to very old music, in its melodic twists, you could say, in combination with sounding modern, if you see what I mean. Many other pieces as well, of course, but these three are especially dear to me!

ARAM: How do you think the music will be heard and remembered by future generations?

ELISABET: Hard to say. It seems that many people get struck by the music. Both those with great knowledge and those who have no earlier connections to so-called classical or contemporary music. It is music written with honesty and the heart, and I think a lot of people feel that. Of course, it demands concentration and time to listen to it. You can't just have it in the background, so it's taxing in a way. But I think people have a need for depth. There is a new need for deeper things I can sense, and many people have lost interest in the superficial, lightweight entertainment that has been the order of the day for so long.

He is not one of those who always pushes himself forward, but he works very slowly and constantly, and he says it must take the time it takes. That, I think, is, in this case anyway, a good sign of quality, and quality often lasts.

ARAM: Do you find it possible to empathize more deeply with Tommie through the music? Have you come to know him in a new way?

ELISABET: My way of handling everything is to mainly look at Tommie as my husband and *not* a composer. If I had to look at him as a composer, it would be impossible to have a normal life.

Nevertheless, I feel very close to his music for many reasons. I love it, I hear him testing things, I play parts of it, I write it on the computer, and so on. But I get very moved every time I listen to something, and sometimes, I don't have the energy to go into it, as it must be listened to with full concentration, and it can stir me up if I'm a little unsettled. I really don't understand how he can do it.

11: THUNDER BAY

Compositions: L'Infinito | Voces

ARAM: Getting back to the spring of 1990, *L'Infinito* was completed around this time.

TOMMIE: Yes. This violinist, Joachim Gustafsson, who has premiered many of my pieces—he has now been a conductor for many years—he asked for a solo violin piece, so I wrote that for him. I had only a week to do it because I misunderstood the dates or something. When he was to record it, we met in the morning at the studio at the Sveriges Radio Broadcasting House in Stockholm. He had a beer at the café, went into the studio, played it once with no stops, all in one take, fifteen minutes straight through—the entire piece. Two takes, maybe, but no edits—a fantastic achievement. Göran W. Nilson, the conductor, was a friend of Joachim's. He said it's a bit like nirvana. And Joachim played that piece at his violin teacher's funeral.[24]

---

24 Joachim Gustafsson's teacher was Eugen Bitto (1930–1992).

ARAM: Something about the piece reminds me of the hypnagogic vision you had in Århus. What is it about, or what is it based upon?

TOMMIE: It's based on a poem by Leopardi.[25] The poem is about sitting in front of a hedge and seeing the sky behind it and not knowing what lies beyond. It's a haunting poem, but it was just the catalyst. I didn't have the poem so much in mind when I wrote it, but *L'Infinito* was also the title of the poem.

Around that time, in fact, I spoke with a specialist named Karin Johannisson, a professor in Uppsala, who wrote a book about hypnagogic states. And actually, she was the girlfriend of Kristoffer Konarski, for whom Elisabet and I wrote this book for Save The Children.[26] Anyway, she wrote an article for the largest newspaper in Sweden about hypnagogic states. I called her up and talked to her about my visions. We had, I think, a one-and-a-half-hour talk. Also, there was a professor of clinical neurophysiology named David Ingvar. We met a couple of times, and we became friends when he was quite old. I told him about this because I wondered

---

25 Giacomo Leopardi (1798–1837) was an Italian lyrical poet and pessimistic philosopher.

26 In 1993, Haglund and his wife Elisabet received funds from the Halmstads Kommun (Council of Halmstad) to develop a pedagogical method for young children involving classical music, with the aim of increasing empathy, imagination, and the ability to concentrate. After meeting Krzysztof Konarski (1947–2001), a professor at the Caroline Institute in Stockholm, they expanded the project to include theories of human emotional development. They subsequently brought the project under the banner of Save the Children, which used the method to care for Bosnian war refugees. A book with a CD was published by Save the Children in 1996.

whether I had some brain damage, and he said, "No, no, no, you just have an extra connection. Be careful with it."

ARAM: What else were you listening to in the late 1980s, after the Jubilee and before you wrote *Voces* and *L'Infinito*?

TOMMIE: Scelsi,[27] whose music made me experience timelessness. Per Nørgård—for intellectual reasons more than emotional. When Victoria was four or five, we went to Copenhagen to see one of his operas. It was broadcast live on Danish television. I was afraid Victoria would get tired and start screaming. Luckily, I had enough candy to keep her happy, and after the performance, Per gave Victoria the balloon that symbolized the spirit. When my first record was released, Per called me and said he was happy with it. When the cello concerto was premiered, he called again and said he didn't like the opening. I asked him why. "Probably because I don't like Bruckner," he said. Stupidly, I made an attempt to re-do the opening, but before the recording with BIS, I went back to the original, and I'm very glad I did. I also studied Arne Mellnäs a great deal, and then I turned to early Medieval composers like Machaut.

ARAM: Dowland, of course.

TOMMIE: Yes, but he was Renaissance, really. Machaut was 1300s. As with Nørgård, this was more of an intellectual pursuit, and it felt necessary to do.

ARAM: Tell me about *Voces*.

---

27 Giacinto Scelsi (1905–1988) was an Italian composer whose works, largely unknown during his lifetime, in retrospect presaged much of postmodern classical music and other microtonal composition. Haglund's interest in Scelsi's work in harmonic allusions and timbral dynamics began after hearing a radio program about him in the late 1980s hosted by Bengt V. Wall (who also wrote a play about Swedenborg, mentioned elsewhere).

TOMMIE: *Voces* was the first piece to involve so many instruments. I expected it to involve too much repetition. And it sounds, I think, like Alban Berg at times—in terms of sonority. Again, there is this anxiety, and I am trying to control brain phantoms. Maybe that's why the piece is repetitive. Almost compulsive repetition. I need to be sure of what I'm saying. Say it once again. Be sure. Sigge Ohlsson commissioned it for the Hallands Ensemble. In retrospect, I think I behaved clumsily with the Hallands Ensemble. I decided to rewrite *Voces* for a large orchestra even after the small ensemble had taken the time to learn it.

ARAM: Schönberg is there as well. It's an expressionistic piece. It somehow manages to be both slow and frenetic at once.

TOMMIE: Expressionistic in the language, yes. Maybe impressionistic as well, at times. I tried to be very careful with the way it was orchestrated. I remember talking to Sven-Eric about it. It's a miscellaneous piece, to be sure. If they're doing a retrospective festival, this piece could represent a period of my work.

ARAM: You were invited to attend a performance of *Voces* and give a lecture on your music in Canada in January of 1991. That was an eventful trip.

TOMMIE: Yes, John Ehde and I had this invitation to visit Canada from Glenn Mossop.[28] So we took a plane to Toronto. They were, as you said, to play *Voces*, and I was to give a lecture at the Music Academy. So, I brought music by Delius and Alban Berg and made comparisons that were very academic. Sometimes, people

---

28 Glenn Mossop (1951–) is a Swedish-Canadian pianist and conductor who was, at the time, chief conductor at the Thunder Bay Symphony Orchestra.

think that Europeans are too academic, so I wore a Mickey Mouse tie. And the first thing I said was that they should write music from the heart. "Begin with the heart, connect it with the brain . . . ." so I talked about that. We were staying in a big house owned by a rich couple. They were Christian Scientists or something. He was a forester. Big house near Lake Ontario. The owners weren't home. We were the only ones there. There was even a grand piano. John and I started drinking too much beer. The first night we arrived, we went immediately to the liquor shop. Lots of beer and crisps. That's how we lived. Anyway, this concert in Thunder Bay took place in a hotel with a restaurant and a big hall sometimes used for concerts. I remember that on the plane, I thought it would be nice to meet someone from the Indigenous population. I was always interested in that as a kid. Lo and behold, after the concert I suddenly found myself in front of a big man who looked like that guy from that Nicholson film. . . what was it?

ARAM: *One Flew Over the Cuckoo's Nest.* Chief.

TOMMIE: Yes. So, I thought, how odd. What does he want? He hadn't realized there was a concert there. He was just in the restaurant. He said he didn't like the first thing, which was Dvorak, but he liked the other thing, which he learned was by me. Said he went up to a mountain called Sleeping Giant for two weeks every year, and the music resembled something about that time for him. This was *Voces*. He had some girl with him. So later, I was at home, and one of the bass players, I think, from the orchestra came there and said, "They want you out on the reservation for a ceremony." This bass player worked for Indigenous rights, an advocate of some kind. "What?" I said. "It's half past nine." He said,

"They want you there now. It takes forty minutes to drive there, so we must go now, and we must also pass a city mall to buy food for you to offer to the spirits." So, I jumped into the car with a jacket and my Mickey Mouse tie. We drove and drove and drove and stopped at this shopping center and bought potatoes, carrots, and cabbage. Then, we entered the reservation and met up with these people with wolf heads. It was amazing!

ARAM: They were Cree?

TOMMIE: Ojibwe, actually. Though the Cree people were living nearby. I realized this was serious, really. They took me down to a basement while the ladies took care of the food. The bass player was with us as well. They said I was to go through what they call a dark room circle, and not even many Ojibwe are allowed to do this, so it was special.

"How long does it take?"

"Three hours."

"I'm going to freeze to death!" It was so cold. They put all the lights out, everything. Then the medicine man came in with dolls and a drum and started to chant and thump the drum. And he said, "Now our forefathers are here."

I saw three flashes. There was something flying over my head. And like that, it was three hours. I didn't know what had happened. Then, they gave me this pipe, and we smoked it, and they burned sweetgrass, and they told me about their religion and how they saw Christianity, their own destiny, and why they had to leave their homes. They said that it was the white man's turn now, that their time had passed. I asked them about the flashes, and they said it was a sign from Manitou. "You are under the protection of the White Eagle." I thought back to what Majken Ohlsson had said five years earlier! So, I got back to the house and was to leave for Sweden. I was to leave a week before John. The orchestra held a big Italian dinner for us, a party with country and western music. [*Laughs.*] I sat next to the managing director of the orchestra, a Danish guy. I still had this pipe with me in a plastic bag. After the meal, I pulled it out and started smoking it. I heard all this murmuring around me. The director turned to me and said, "Do you know what they smoke in that pipe? Squirrel shit. Not tobacco." I answered that it was first-class tobacco. Then this country and western band started, and it was a country dance. God, I hated it.

ARAM: How . . . authentic.

TOMMIE: They had interviewed me on Canadian Radio that day. It was broadcast all over Ontario. "So," the commentator asked me, "Is there anything you're inspired by here in Canada?" I said, "No, not particularly." "Nature?" "No, not really. Oh," I said, "there is one thing. It's about this situation with the First Nations. They're certainly not first nations. They're not even second. They're more like third rate members of society here."

"And now, Bob Dylan"—that's how it ended.

ARAM: [*Laughs.*] Is that what they did?

TOMMIE: Yes, I was sent off from the radio station in a taxi with a beer. The Ojibwe people had heard the radio broadcast and came and found me at that Italian dinner with the country-western band. There was a pow-wow at the Reservation. They asked if I would come get in the car. So, we went back to the Reservation. There were hundreds of Ojibwe and two big drums. The chief came up to me and said, "I think you shall dance, Tommie." It felt

Photos: Jennifer Garrett

This page and next, Tommie Haglund with members of the Ojibwe Tribe, Thunder Bay, Canada, 1991.

much more natural to dance there than to this country and western stuff. It was really fantastic, but also really strange. I was one of them now. They gave me some cassette tapes of them singing and playing the drums. And also, the chief gave me a set of dolls representing the yellow man, the white man, the red man, and the black man. I was to place them in a tree. "Leave there until they're gone," he said. So, I did. The Canadians said this was so unusual. They really made a profound impact on me.

ARAM: That does not happen to everyone.

TOMMIE: I'll never, ever forget it. Here I am in a Mickey Mouse tie. I'm this very silly European with a silly tie to provoke the composition students. They asked me to join a sweat lodge with them, but there just wasn't time. I had to leave. It still baffles me that I had this experience.

ARAM: What part of *Voces* do you think reminded that Ojibwe fellow of his time on the mountain?

TOMMIE: It's a question I've asked myself many times. It's quite European in attitude.

ARAM: Maybe we shouldn't think about it academically. Who knows what he heard in it or what we hear in it? There is an up-and-away feel to it. Some passages felt like something floating away or birds taking flight, voices rising up. Maybe he tuned into that.

TOMMIE: I really wanted to say something with that piece. It's lonely music. Solitude. Maybe that's what he felt.

12: GREZ-SUR-LOING, FRANCE

ARAM: What happened when you returned to Sweden?

TOMMIE: In the autumn of 1990 I received a call from an American singer who was a coloratura soprano. She'd sung the lead role in *The Phantom of the Opera* in Vienna. Her name is Janet Chvatal, and she was a friend of John Ehde's. She'd heard my music played in Paris or something. I really don't know in what context. But she was very enthusiastic and wanted me to write a piece for soprano, violin, cello, and piano, where her voice would be treated as an instrument, so there would be no text. She was very virtuosic and could hit any note without difficulty. So, I got together with Joachim Gustafsson—who commissioned *L'Infinito*—John Ehde, Christen Stubbe Teglbjærg, and Janet. I began writing what was to be *Miraggio* even before I went to Canada, and—I think it was in March 1991—I went up to Örebro to meet Joachim. We did all this work and then had a big party. Stefan Lindgren was there as well. We were drinking rather heavily, a bit more than I could take. I had not written anything down. The music was all in my head. On the train back to Halmstad the next day, I couldn't remember a thing. Not one note. I called Elisabet from a pay phone and said, "What am I going to do? I can't remember! It's all gone. It's all gone!" She said, "Well, it'll come back if it's worth anything." But it didn't. And Janet was to come in a few days!

ARAM: Janet was coming to Halmstad to learn her part, and you had nothing?

TOMMIE: Yes! I had nothing for several days, and then the day before she arrived, I had a very high fever . . . and the music came back! But I had a really high temperature. So, I sat in the music room, which was a rebuilt garage in my old house. It had a big window. I sat there, writing it out, and I saw out the window a cliff of gold, rising up, with a face of gold staring at me. And there were colors radiating from the top. The whole sky turned into silver. It was a fever vision. It wasn't frightening, so I kept writing. It was very similar to what happened in Århus. Sometimes, I can see pictures that look like Islamic geometric art or mandalas. Impossible to describe.

I picked up Janet at the station the next evening. My piano was out of tune, so we went to the university. We played it through, and she liked it. The next day, my fever was higher, and I was in bed for the whole week. She was there for eight days, and I was in bed. Somehow, we managed to get the piece together, and it was premiered here at an international music festival. Lots of musicians were coming from Russia and all over. The festival was shortly after I returned from Canada, so parts of the composition I actually wrote in Canada, in my head. But after this fever, I began to feel back pain. The pain became immense. And my marriage with

Helen was crashing down at that point. The stress I was under—and also Helen—at this time was immense. My two girls were my biggest worry.

ARAM: You were still with Helen at this point?

TOMMIE: Yes. This was 1991, and the music was expressing the immense anxiety I was feeling. But Helen and I had just bought—actually built—this new house out in the country—a house I didn't want to own. It cost an enormous amount of money. More money than I could earn. Those were really harrowing years. I didn't want to play the guitar anymore, and yet I had almost no hope of writing music. And there were no more university positions. I had no idea at that point that I could become a full-time composer. And the marriage was breaking apart. I felt terrible because of that, mostly for my children. But there was nothing I could do. There was nothing—nothing I could do. I thought that I didn't want my children to grow up in a cold marriage. It was the hardest decision I ever made.

ARAM: But also, at this time, you were starting to enjoy a certain success.

TOMMIE: That's right. There was much more attention than there ever had been—more than I ever dreamed of, really. I didn't hesitate to go into arguments with people. For example, Joachim was the artistic director of a string quintet and a wind quintet, ten players in all who were fired one day from Musik i Halland by a new musical director. He wanted freelance musicians instead. I was quoted in the newspaper as saying he'd had an artistic brain hemorrhage. And that caused an enormous stir. He called me in and really laid into me in front of a number of people. I explained I didn't mean his personal brain. What did I know about that? It was just the decision he'd made that was a hemorrhage. And he should know better than to call me in here. And there was dead silence. Maybe I said too much? I had so much confidence, but I wasn't really happy. It was also a time when I was meeting many world-class musicians. But if I'd known what was to come, I don't know if I could have faced it.

ARAM: Am I correct in thinking this was just before you and Elisabet visited Grez-sur-Loing? That was a very important mission you went on.

TOMMIE: Yes, it was.

ARAM: Theodore Pitcairn, whom we've discussed with reference to Soldanella, and Delius both had estates at Grez-sur-Loing at the same time. Soldanella's father, Philip Oyler, managed Pitcairn's estate there. For him to have managed the estate and for Soldanella and Fenby to have met, it's difficult to believe Theo and Delius weren't themselves acquainted.

TOMMIE: Yes. Oh yes. He visited Delius at least once according to Soldanella. You see, Delius and Jelka[29] had Gaugin's *Nevermore* hanging in the house—Delius and Gaugin were friends when they were younger. But during the depression, they lost money and had to sell it, along with the house, to Balfour Gardiner, a relative of John Eliot Gardiner's. Before they did, Jelka made a copy of it. Theo came to see the copy. This is what Soldanella told me. She

---

29 Jelka Rosen (1868–1935) was a painter and wife of Delius, whose independent wealth allowed the composer a measure of financial security.

Photo: unknown

Frederick Delius and Jelka Delius in their garden at Grez-sur-Loing, ca. 1916.

went there many times because, as you say, Philip Oyler ran the estate for Theo.

We went there, to Grez, Elisabet and I, and got engaged on the bridge. This was the summer of 1993. And we decided to find the Pitcairn estate, Château les Pleignes. It was very difficult to find.

ARAM: Someone else made the same comment to me about trying to find Theo's estate in Grez. They said they nearly gave up looking after hours and then finally found it by accident.

TOMMIE: We found Theo's estate. We found it; Elisabet and I did. I'll tell you; it was like trying to find the castle in *Sleeping Beauty*. Everything had grown up around it. But we were there. It was not inhabited by anyone. No one owned it. It just stood there. Trees growing all over. We had to fight our way in. Pitcairn built it in the style of the old châteaus, but not really French, somehow. The people there didn't consider it to be a nice house, meaning, not authentically French. He must have been immensely rich in those days to have built such a thing. I'd like to go there and try to find it again. It was really like going into a dream.

ARAM: Did you go inside?

TOMMIE: No. The gate was locked. That was our first summer together, Elisabet and I. We'd just bought a new car, a Mitsubishi Space Wagon. The children were away, and it was pouring rain here. We thought we'd just get out of here and leave for France. I suggested we go to Grez-sur-Loing. So, we just drove down there in the rain. We drove down through Germany, through Holland. When we came to Grez, I put on a tape of Delius' *In a Summer Garden*. We played it, and just as the music was reaching its climax, I looked to the left, and there was Delius' house! Elisabet will tell you; it's just exactly what happened. And then, I wanted to stay where Percy Grainger[30] and all Delius' guests had stayed. So, we booked into this old hotel that hadn't been renovated since the '30s. It was dirty, filthy, creepy, and the owners were alcoholics. The beds were like pits. You had to hold onto the posts to avoid sliding into the middle. The place seemed like it hadn't been cleaned since Grainger slept there. We stayed there one night, and Elisabet refused to sleep there a second night. And it was Bastille Day, so

---

30 Percy Grainger (1882–1961) was an Australian-born composer and pianist who sustained a long friendship with Delius. He was a frequent guest at the Delius households in both Norway and France.

everyone was drunk. And we could barely get to the room because a black collie was guarding the hallway. I didn't really mind. In the morning, I wanted to go out and find some lithographs of Delius' house. The lady couldn't understand us properly, so she called to her neighbor on the opposite side of the street. They lived at the house next to Delius' and spoke perfect English. We didn't find any lithographs, so the daughter of the house, Marie-Laurence, asked would we like to meet her family. We went into this house, a rebuilt barn with high ceilings—very posh inside. The owner said he'd been the managing director of IBM in France. He must have been one of the richest men in the country. He'd made his money during the Vietnam War. He'd been raised by an English governess, and he was so fascinated that I was a composer. One of the comments he made was, "Musicians never start wars." He took a liking to us, really. And he said, "Look, I've got postcards, around eight hundred postcards from the middle of the 1800s to 1970." A huge album with all these postcards. I promise now. I just flipped it open and took out one card, and it said, *Hello from Philip Oyler*!

ARAM: To whom?

TOMMIE: It didn't say, or I can't remember. It was the first card I took! Elisabet saw me. I turned completely white in the face.

ARAM: Why is he at the center of so many coincidences?

TOMMIE: Yes, I don't know. Why is he turning up at every corner? Out of eight hundred cards, I picked out this one. Unbelievable. Well, anyway, I'd had the commission for the cello concerto by then, so I started thinking about that while we were there. Our host was a colonialist, he said. I thought he was joking. He sympathized with Le Pen, which was quite unusual in those days.

ARAM: Did he indeed?

TOMMIE: In those days, we really didn't know Le Pen. It was just a name. It's something I see as very dangerous now, but back then, we didn't know. But in another sense, he—our host—was the softest man I'd ever met. And his best friend across the street was some kind of left-wing socialist. Really strange. He could say some strange things. Like they said Elisabet was the perfect Norman woman. He served champagne, foie gras, everything. Before we could react, Henri phoned a Vietnamese friend in Nemour and made a reservation for later in the week. We went there a few days later and had one of the best meals I've had in my life, really. The food was decorated like art. Especially the julienned carrots around the fish.

But anyway, the second evening, Elisabet and I checked into a new hotel in Bourron, the neighboring village, but for the rest of the week, we were back in Grez living at a bed-and-breakfast owned by Henri's socialist friend. We took a walk one evening to the edge of the village and saw a man standing, watering his flowers. Lots of flowers. We looked at them and said it was very nice. He asked where we were from.

"From Sweden. I'm a composer and this is my wife," I said. "We're interested in Delius."

"Oh," he said. "I have a painting of Delius' house inside. Would you like to come in?"

So, we went in. He said he had been a restaurant owner in Sacré-Cœur, a chef. He introduced us to his wife. We had some foie gras, pink champagne. We were talking to them about everything and saw the painting of Delius' house. He was seventy-five or something.

He said, "If you come tomorrow, I'll cook you a real French dinner. And I'll take you to a place where you can buy some really good wine." We misunderstood him. We thought he meant we would get the wine first and then eat, so at lunchtime, we had spaghetti with some cream, carbonara or something, and a bottle of wine.

We were sitting outside, and his wife came and said, "It's time for dinner." So, we went to the house. It was champagne again, foie gras, snails, fish vol-au-vent, white wine sauce, a good white wine, a partridge with mushrooms and a red wine sauce, potatoes au gratin, and red wine. After that, there was cheese and another red wine. And then cake and some dessert wine. We were completely drunk! We made it to the place to buy the wine. I don't know how, but we did. When we got back to the house, we just fell down and went to sleep, laughing. That evening we were supposed to go to a party at Henri's house—the man with the postcards—and we made it there, barely. Later, we went back to see this restaurant owner, whose name was Nassier. He was really very warm-hearted, and I said to him, "Fenby, when Delius so wished, would row him on the river Loing, the river which goes to Delius' house." Nassier's house was also on the river.

So, he said, "Well, I haven't got a boat, but my neighbor has one." So, he rushed off to his neighbor and asked if we could borrow the boat, and Elisabet and I went out on this boat, on the river, and rowed all the way to Delius' house. We got engaged on the bridge that day. It was one of those rare moments where time seemed to stand still. On the same bridge Eric and Soldanella got engaged—they were secretly engaged. I dropped an oar that day, also.

ARAM: Were you able to enter Delius' house?

Photo: Elisabet Löfberg Haglund

Bridge, Grez-sur-Loing, France, ca. 1993

TOMMIE: No, there was no one there. So, we decided to come back. Henri had bought a house for his daughter from Prince Romanov. He said we could borrow it the next time we came. So, we went back to Grez two summers later with the children and stayed two weeks. They took care of us so well. Victoria and I went into Delius' house and garden. It was magical to walk in the house and garden with my daughter. We were again invited to dine with Monsieur Nassier and his wife. This time it was duck with fried potatoes and a bit less wine. Monsieur Nassier said he felt like a father to us. When we returned home, we got a touching letter from him. He had been quite badly treated during the war as a member of the Resistance. Fenby describes Grez-sur-Loing very well in his book. Apart from cars, it hasn't changed much since he wrote about it. I called Fenby from a phone box the first time we were in

Grez. He was very old and tired then. It took five minutes for him to get to the phone. He wanted to know what it looked like then. Nothing changed. It was the last time I talked to him.

ARAM: Is that right?

TOMMIE: Yes, a few years later, in 1997, we had gone to Istanbul for a weekend, and when I returned, I had this urge to listen to Delius' violin concerto. After that, I phoned Eric, and his daughter answered. We spoke for a while, and she said she'd been taking care of her father. I said, "Well, may I speak to him?"

"Well," she said, "he just died just a few hours ago."

13: INIM-INIM

ARAM: The next significant piece you completed after the trip to Grez and getting engaged to Elisabet was *Inim-Inim*. This is a piece that has fascinated many people. Its hermeticism is not something typical for you, and nothing else sounds quite like it. What kind of ideas and experiences inspired it?

TOMMIE: It's a mysterious thing: what set in motion the creative process in the universe? Was it a sound? Did God speak a word, and then it unfolded? Did vibrations ignite the whole thing? Swedenborg is talking about tremulations, which has a certain connection to string theory. To me, it's the same mystery as how some music can create a tension in the room—*Stimmung*.[31] There must be an immense power for people to be reduced to tears by music. It was this mystery I was pondering when I wrote *Inim-Inim*. It's very abstract music, one of my most abstract pieces. I never

31 *Stimmung* is a German word that encapsulates both the tuning of an instrument and the mood elicited from the tuning.

turned back to that way of writing again. I wanted it to be multidimensional. When you listen to it, you can pinpoint certain places where I thought very much of Machaut.[32] He was a diplomat and poet and also wrote the first Mass ever, with Kyrie, Gloria, Sanctus, Benedictus, Agnus Dei, and everything. What captured me with Machaut was the rhythm, the syncopations, and isorhythms so common in those days. But also how much weight he laid on dissonance that doesn't dissolve into consonance. Of course, that's connected with his research of sonorous tensions—something he often used in his compositional technique.

Sometimes, the theories take over, and the symmetries and balance themselves become the goal, more than how the music sounds. It isn't dissimilar to the serialists in that way.

With *Inim-Inim,* there aren't melodic quotations, but there are parts where I thought very much about Machaut, and I felt there were intersections, particularly in the first movement of his Mass. I was reading lots of Rosicrucian literature during that time. I really don't know why. Sven had given me some texts, particularly by Harvey Spencer Lewis, and I found these very interesting. I could easily accept what he wrote. And I found in it a mysticism that was not so . . . pretentious. Another way of looking inwards. Deeper. A kind of side-track to Swedenborg, really.

ARAM: And one not completely unrelated.

---

32 Guillaume de Machaut (c. 1300–1377) was a French Medieval lyric poet and composer of both sacred and secular music.

TOMMIE: No, no, right. That piece was about going as far out into the universe, or into your own universe—it's the same thing. Here Machaut comes in again, and the metaphysical thinking of that time. In one of his rounds, *Ma fin est mon commencement* (My End is My Beginning), he uses retrogrades—pitches and rhythms playing forward and then in reverse: the thought of life as circular and death as the start of rebirth. There might be solutions inside us to the questions of our existence, or is there a limit to how much we can take? I was also thinking a great deal about our small existence in this enormous cosmos and how little we know. Time both exists and doesn't exist. *Inim-Inim* ends on the wrong note. You think it should end with a B, but it ends with an A. And it changes your perception about the solution to the structure. I worked on that piece for a long time. All these chords were hovering in my head. I wanted the sense of pulse to vanish. I wanted it to be free. It's not easy listening. I remember I had a hell of a time putting it down on paper, notating it, and grasping the chord progression. It's not even published yet as a score.

ARAM: Mysticism—I don't want to say it's a nothing word, but it can mean just about anything. What does it mean to you, beyond a way of tying up loose questions in your life?

TOMMIE: I think it's going into secret rooms in your most inner self—to have a room that is indestructible. To me it's about coming close to the divine that is always around us, but it demands silence and stillness. Beethoven kept a quotation on his desk; I often think about it. It was about the divine as something you can't grasp: "I am that which is. I am all that was, that is, and that shall be. No mortal man has ever lifted the veil of me. He is solely of himself, and to this Only One all things owe their existence."[33]

ARAM: Such things are difficult to access with language.

TOMMIE: You know they're there, but you don't know how to reach them. And suddenly, you find the key. You go in, and you just need to go further and further. And some of these rooms are very frightening—those are the ones I've been experiencing quite a lot, with the violin concerto and the cello concerto. I've been trying to reach the most painful, the most frightening things, the saddest things I ever can think of, and just clean them out.

ARAM: To name it is to know it—to have power over it.

TOMMIE: Exactly. There's a word for that here: *åkallan*. What is it in English? Invocation.

ARAM: And yet, with the music, when you invoke terror and sadness, even as fraudulent, don't you risk giving these things lives of their own?

TOMMIE: I expose them to myself.

ARAM: And yourself to them.

TOMMIE: I still wake up in panics when I'm composing. They last all through breakfast and then vanish when I sit down in the music room and write.

ARAM: Have you ever felt like any of your work was inauthentic or fraudulent?

---

33 Stephen Ley, ed., *Beethovens Leben in authentischen Bildern und Texten* (Berlin: B. Cassirer, 1925), 129. According to Holmqvist, Beethoven sourced this quote from Champollion's *The Paintings of Egypt* where it is said to have been sourced, in turn, from an inscription in a temple to the goddess Neith. Beethoven framed the quote and kept it on his desk.

TOMMIE: No, not anything I've completed. Never, never, never, never, never, never, never, never, never. Oh no. If it's not really me, it goes in the bin. I need so much time to place every note where it should be. There was this old musicologist, Bo Wallner, who was a member of the Monday Group with Blomdahl. He wrote in a review about the *Inim-Inim* CD, which has *Intenso Animi* on it, in which he pointed out the loneliness of it. A very difficult track. He said he could achieve a hallucinatory state through the music, but he wondered whether I could go on and what else I'd achieve with it. I took that quite seriously.

ARAM: *Inim-Inim* has a 3D quality, which makes it cinematic for me. I mean, when I listen to Bach and Haydn, I don't have any automatic visual sense for anything, but with *Inim-Inim* I do.

TOMMIE: There are so many things going on in *Inim-Inim* simultaneously. Rhythms, syncopation, parallel structures—fast and slow at the same time. That may be why you have to hang it on something visual. I wrote *Inim-Inim* without bar lines. Dan Almgren[34] put them in afterward, but when I wrote it, there were no bar lines because I wanted it to be completely free. Sometimes the piano and violin are playing independently of each other, but it still all fits. Some critics said it was hard to even find a pulse because there were so many things happening. If you saw it written down, you'd think it was difficult, whereas the cello concerto actually looks dead easy on paper but isn't so easy to play.

---

34 Dan Almgren (1961–) is a Swedish violinist and one of the founders of Stockholm Arts Trio.

ARAM: How can you notate something with this kind of complexity?

TOMMIE: The music is in the air, and it just comes to me. But it's sometimes difficult to get it on paper when details are moving around. The day after you hear something new, and you know it fits, but it's threading the eye of a tiny needle. I think I'm writing a bit simpler now, so it looks simpler on paper, but I don't think that means less quality. But soon after *Inim-Inim,* things really came crashing down. I was taken seriously ill. I was in immense pain. In a matter of a few weeks everything had changed forever.

14: MORTALITY

Compositions: Spirarae Celourum | Kärlekshjärtan

ARAM: You said that after *Inim-Inim,* life changed forever. What was the source of that change?

TOMMIE: A herniated disc. Spasms of shaking. They'd come once, sometimes twice in a day, and took a lot of strength from me. When I began medication, I couldn't remember anything . . . apart from music. The music, I could remember every note. But little else. Many times, I was in town and couldn't find my way home. I had to call Elisabet to come and find me because I did not know where I was. I couldn't remember phone numbers, and I was used to having an exceptional memory. When Elizabeth Pitcairn[35] was here recording the violin concerto, there was an ambulance standing outside the Helsingborg Symphony Orchestra's Hall. The pain and mental states were that bad.

---

35 Elizabeth Pitcairn (1973–) is an American solo violinist who commissioned Haglund's *Hymnen an die Nacht* and premiered it on CD.

ARAM: When did the pain begin?

TOMMIE: Around 1990, I helped my father move house, which meant carrying a lot of furniture. After driving home and standing up from the car, I felt a pain in my back, and over the years, it grew worse, but it didn't take over my life until August of 1995. This was when Elisabet and I returned from Grez-sur-Loing the second time—when we took the girls. That summer in August, we held a big party. Soldanella was there. It was a crayfish party with lots of people. And I remember that I didn't feel well at all in my back. A few months later in the autumn, Elisabet and I were to hold a sort of seminar in Halmstad. This was for our Save the Children project. It was a UN Day thing, I believe. That morning, I collapsed on the floor of the shower and couldn't stand back up. Elisabet called for the neighbor, who was a military man, a big fellow. He lifted me up, but I couldn't stand. So he called for an ambulance, and I was taken to the hospital. This very nonchalant, half-educated Danish doctor came in. He wasn't even a doctor yet, I don't think. He said, "Well, there's nothing wrong with you." He didn't order X-rays. Instead, he made a comment about me lacking muscle in my lower back. "I'll give you a few pills, and you can go home." So, I went back and actually held the seminar on these painkillers. And then, at night, I said to Elisabet, "It feels like something is pouring out inside my back." She phoned the hospital, and they said to come in the morning, early. In the morning, I had to take an ambulance to the hospital. My legs were going numb. They said either it's a tumor or, in the best case, it's a herniated disc. If so, you'll be fine within nine weeks. They made an X-ray. I was so nervous. It did turn out to be a herniated disc, and I was so relieved!

ARAM: Relieved about a herniated disc!

TOMMIE: Yes, because it was not a tumor. But I was still in immense pain. A few days before, I'd had a dream that I was in a garden, emerald green, but drenched in tears. I asked someone where I was, and they told me it was Gethsemane. I woke up and knew something bad was going to happen. Three days later, they called for an operation on my back. Something happened. It didn't take place at the appointed time, and I had to wait another twenty-four hours. I was in such pain that they had to put me to sleep. I couldn't lie still. When I woke up from the operation, I was numb from the waist down. I asked one of the nurses, "When will the sensation come back?" She asked, "What do you mean? The anesthesia has gone away. You're awake." I said I needed to talk to the doctor. The doctor came in and said the nerves might come back; they might not come back. Meanwhile, I can't walk, I can't do anything. I was helpless. I was on as much morphine and painkillers as I could take. I lay there for three weeks, four weeks, five weeks, seven weeks. One day, I just broke down and forced myself up and used a walker. I took the elevator down to the street but collapsed. Then the elevator broke down, and they couldn't get me back upstairs for an hour.

ARAM: What hospital was this? The one across the street here?

TOMMIE: Yes. But of course, we weren't living here yet. We lived in the country at that point. I stayed there a total of seven weeks. I had to use two braces. After I returned home, I was alone in the daytime. Elisabet used to leave sandwiches for me, but I couldn't sit and could barely eat them. I had to lay flat in the car, and of course, I could not drive myself.

ARAM: What did you do during those years?

TOMMIE: All I did was compose, read Swedenborg, and watch *Laurel and Hardy* and *Fawlty Towers*. I couldn't help my children as much as I wanted to—I couldn't be there for them.

ARAM: When did the panic attacks start?

TOMMIE: The first panic attack came before Christmas 1995. This was just after I got home from hospital—after the operation. I walked into a big grocery store with Elisabet. She hadn't wanted me to go in, but I went anyway. Immediately my heart started beating at 180–200, and I had tunnel vision, my arms became numb. I couldn't breathe. Just by coincidence, there was a nurse standing there. "You're hyperventilating," she said. And I just fell down. The ambulance came. I didn't know what was happening. I remember asking them if it was alright to breathe. We got to the hospital, and the doctor arrived. Just a panic attack, he said. Nothing wrong. He gave me sedative pills. What were those things called? Bens... Benz...

ARAM: Benzodiazepine.

TOMMIE: Yes, so I was fine the next day. Day after that, another panic attack. And these started to occur frequently. I think they were echoes of all the things that had happened: the broken marriage, childhood, everything just crashing down. And, you know, the day before the operation, I had a call from Carl-Axel Dominique[36] saying

---

36 Carl-Axel Dominique (1939–) is a Swedish pianist and composer well known for his interpretations of Olivier Messiaen's piano works. He has performed *Inim-Inim, Mirragio, Intensio Animi, Daughter of the Voice,* and others of Haglund's pieces for recording, as well as premiered several pieces of his chamber music.

I'd been commissioned to write a piece for the King of Sweden's fiftieth birthday.

ARAM: Which piece was that?

TOMMIE: That was the clavisino piece, *Spirarae Celourum*.

ARAM: This was still 1995?

TOMMIE: Yes. I wrote *Spirarae Celourum* in bed, in the hospital, after the operation on my back. Finally, after months, I was able to do lectures again. I even wrote the cello concerto lying down. At the same time, I was receiving commissions—first from the Medici Quartet to write a string quartet for their 30th Jubilee.

ARAM: How did that come about?

TOMMIE: It was through Gunilla von Bahr.[37] She met me and wondered if I had written a string quartet. She offered to send something to Paul Robertson[38] from the Medici Quartet, and he phoned me and asked me to compose for them. The quartet was to be premiered in connection with their 30th Jubilee, in connection with the Cambridge Chamber Music Festival. I received money from the Baltic Sea Festival for this commission. It's dedicated to Elisabet and in memory of Soldanella, who had died. Composing was what kept me going at that time. I gave a three-hour lecture at Trinity College at Cambridge, flying on strong medication. I was to talk about creativity and death. I was present for the rehearsals of the quartet and everything. The BBC interviewed me.

---

37 Gunilla von Bahr (1941–2013) was a Swedish flutist and headmaster of the Swedish Royal Academy in Stockholm, and former wife of Robert von Bahr, who owns BIS Records.

38 Paul Robertson (1952–2016) was the first violinist in the Medici Quartet, who also published a book about near-death experiences, *Soundscapes: A Musician's Journey Through Life and Death*.

Paul and I met at his house in Surrey with Peter Fenwick,[39] who researched near-death experiences. David Ignatius was there, too. We talked a lot about music, mysticism, and Swedenborg. Anyway, this is what would become the string quartet, *Il Regno degli Spiriti*. I remember I wrote a lot of the quartet outside in the winter while it was freezing. I was obsessed for some reason with drinking tomato juice with Tabasco in it—in the middle of the night. And I started smoking. The quartet was performed in the Royal Palace in Stockholm. And Göran Appelgren arranged for it to be performed in the Swedenborgian Church. In an interview with Swedish Radio P-2, Paul was asked if the piece could be compared with anything, and he answered the only thing he could think of was one of Beethoven's late quartets. This embarrassed me, but I let it stand.

ARAM: Anyway, getting back to *Spirarae Celourum*. This piece was written for the King of Sweden.

TOMMIE: Yes, that was a commission for the King's birthday. It's the most un-festive piece of music I've ever written in my life.

ARAM: Un-festive for you or the King?

TOMMIE: For the King. By un-festive, I mean it's not celebratory. It's introverted music. It's a piece for a King, meant to give him—and other listeners—time to look inwards.

ARAM: So, it's not particularly bombastic.

TOMMIE: No! It's quarter-tones and stuff like that. And he really liked it! [*Laughs.*] It's for clavichord, actually a clavisino, a

39 Peter Fenwick (1935–2024) was a British neuropsychologist, well known for his studies of near-death experiences and a studied belief that human consciousness may be more than simply brain function.

Photo: unknown

Tommie Haglund receiving His Majesty The King's Medal from King Carl XVI Gustaf and Queen Silvia of Sweden, 2015.

unique amplified clavichord made by Joel Jedström.[40] Carl-Axel Dominique premiered the piece.

ARAM: Were you even thinking about the King when you wrote it?

TOMMIE: No! I was thinking about a scale with sixteen notes because he's Carl the Sixteenth, but then I thought that was ludicrous. So, I ended up working with quarter-tones. I started composing it in bed five days after the operation for my herniated disc. I was in terrible shape. I couldn't carry on at home, so I was sent to a sanatorium for exercise. It was an old-fashioned place a bit further north from here. I remember lying there and writing it in my room. Gradually, the nerve sensation in my legs was coming

40 Joel Jedström, Swedish instrument builder.

back, so I'd try to make it out to the dining room to play a few notes on the piano. I wrote that piece there. I actually met Sven-Eric's wife, Karin. She was resting there as well. And there was a piano there. I used to go and play one note, then a few notes—just to have contact with something—then a chord.

Anyway, I would like to orchestrate *Spirarae Celourum* or perhaps make a version for organ. I would be very interested to see what happens. Otherwise, it's just a piece on the periphery. But I wanted to do my utmost best for this piece, not least because it was for the King. Bengt-Emil Johnson[41] played it on the radio and said, "This is really 'royal' music" or something. [*Laughs.*]

ARAM: There are these extended notes in *Spirarae* that are like raga and La Monte Young,[42] though not quite as extended as that.

TOMMIE: Right! Very much so. Interesting you say that. You know, there's an even more bizarre version of it with different microphone placement, and it became quite different. It sounded like an amplified sitar.

ARAM: That same year, you wrote a double round called *Kärlekshjärtan.*

TOMMIE: It's based on a poem by Amanda, my youngest daughter. First, it's an ordinary round for two violins. Then, there's a theme, and the theme goes backward; a new theme, backward.

---

41 Bengt Emil Johnson (1936–2010) was a Swedish composer, concrete poet, radio broadcaster, and a central figure in art scenes such as Fylkingen and Pistolteatern.

42 La Monte Young (1935–) is an American composer and pioneer of minimalism and drone music. "Extended notes" is a reference to Young's practice of sustained tones or just intonation. Young himself was interested in and inspired by the *alap* section of the Indian Classical raga cycle.

Two bars, one phrase, and then the same phrase backward. And again. Strict counterpoint. And the whole thing at half speed, all together, so two rounds put together, backward and forward. She only let me use the white keys.

ARAM: I take it the backward sections were live, not you looping them electronically.

TOMMIE: No, no, that was a live performance.

ARAM: This was a tone poem or prose?

TOMMIE: Prose. She wrote it when she was three or four: "Love hearts. Love hearts. Bouncing ball around in a ring. The butterfly flies so beautifully. Hardly I can die, hardly I can die. And strawberries." What a sensitive little girl. But also very strong-willed and full of absurd humor. When she got older, and I was to say goodnight, she made up very imaginative stories.

The recording is children, young teenagers with string orchestra and percussion and piano. It's in a big church. I knew the conductor, so we put it together and did it. It was a commission from Kulturskolan.[43] This was the first piece I wrote after the commission for the King, and I wanted to see if I could sharpen myself up intellectually after all that had happened. I was constantly tired and in doubt about my capacities.

---

43 Kulturskolan is an institution for publicly financed education for children in collaboration with the Swedish Ministry of Education.

15: ARCANA

Compositions: Arcana Lacrimae | Varsamt, Victoria sover | Daughter of the Voice

ARAM: The next year you started work on a major piece, *Arcana Lacrimae.*

TOMMIE: It's a bit like the Delius *Arabesque.* I was walking on a path I'd never taken. It feels different from everything else. I wanted to see what I could do with a different palate. The title is *Tears in Secret,* of course. The secrets are things you can't talk about, things you can't find the words for. I wrote it when we were moving house, and I completed it while staying with friends for a few weeks, waiting for the new house. I was very anxiety-ridden and in a lot of pain. It didn't take long to write that piece. It's a very atonal work. Some minor thirds returning as an echo of tonality and references to Dowland.

ARAM: The title is seemingly a Swedenborg reference.

TOMMIE: There is this mystery with Swedenborg's texts. *Arcana.* Secrets. I wanted to put that in another context and combine it with the mysteries of Dowland. The former was an intellectual enigma, the latter an emotional enigma.

ARAM: Who was the pianist?

TOMMIE: Hans Pålsson. He recorded for BIS. He's premiered, I think, 150 works and is a very well-known TV personality. Huge knowledge of Beethoven and the Austrian-German Classical style, among others, but not at all French, not at all Messiaen. I didn't know how he was going to react to the piece. I thought he'd consider it just another modern piece by a young Swedish upstart composer. Luckily, he was thrilled by it and wanted me to write a letter about the music to him. I didn't realize it was for a book he was working on.

ARAM: Pålsson was the one who made the comment about dream logic.

TOMMIE: Yes, he's talking about that in the television documentary.[44] *Arcana* was written for him to play. He commissioned it for a festival and wrote about it in his book—he got an award for that book—a whole chapter about that piece. He has a very good explanation of it. It's also published in *Arte,* the Royal Swedish Academy's journal.

ARAM: I'm reading here from the book, which is in Swedish: "His work is not a cheap decoration, nor a search for effects, but dares to sink itself in, all the way down to the heart."[45] He later

---

44 Pålsson appeared in a 2013 episode of *Själens musik* (Music of the Soul), a Swedish documentary series produced by Nicolas Linde and Mikael Persson for SVT2 that delves into the intersection of music and personal narratives, exploring how music influences and reflects the human experience.

45 Hans Pålsson, *Tankar om musik* (Stockholm: Prisma, 2002), 45.

quotes another critic saying, "It was like hearing music for the first time ever." That's as much a compliment as one could ever hope to receive.

TOMMIE: On the other hand, one of the reviewers said it was the worst piece of music he'd ever heard in his life. (Then, ten years later, the same piece was played by the same pianist, and the same reviewer compared it to the late piano works of Brahms.) [*Laughs.*] You mustn't read these things too often. You lose sight of yourself. Pålsson himself didn't record it; Stefan Lindgren[46] did. He's a member of the Royal Stockholm Philharmonic Orchestra. He's an exceptional pianist. He wrote me an email saying perhaps he'd played it too fast in some sections for the recording. But I think his playing was exquisite. Many others have done their own interpretations.

ARAM: I'll probably have to listen to it two or three times more before I can really let it flow. What was going on?

TOMMIE: You tell me.

ARAM: There were parts that felt opaque. It's unusual. Usually, I know what you're up to. [*Laughs.*] There was some high-octave and low-octave stuff together that was marvelous, and I don't know if it's Stefan Lindgren's proclivity to stab with the keys or if you prescribed that, but he was doing it. You know, there was some rumbling like water running over rocks and then stabbing—what a contrast, but we haven't made it to the heart of the work. There

---

46 Stefan Lindgren (1960–) is a Swedish pianist who studied at Musikhögskolan i Stockholm and later at Juilliard in New York. He is a soloist with most of the major orchestras in Sweden and several abroad.

were sometimes notes that were almost untouched, so soft . . . and I thought, maybe that was an error, or . . .

TOMMIE: No, no!

ARAM: . . . or some incredible control! There was a motif that seemed to disappear and then pick up again, just where it left off.

TOMMIE: I'm surprised each time I hear it, and there are things I like about it—I don't dislike it—but it was a sidetrack for me, that piece, in a way. It was a track I never followed further.

ARAM: The cello concerto wasn't completed until 2001, but its life began at least six years earlier, even before the piece for the King. Is that right?

TOMMIE: Yes, in 1995, I think. Göran Bergendahl, who was working at Swedish Radio and was involved with commissions at the Rikskonserter—and thus had power over musical life in Sweden at the time. He was to introduce my music at a concert for radio broadcast. We did an interview before the concert, and he asked me whether I considered myself to be an outsider. I said no, but I have a feeling that's what he thought. After that, he said he thought it was time for a more substantial commission. He was the one who commissioned *Inim-Inim*, so now he was suggesting something with full orchestra. I couldn't believe it. I asked what he had in mind, and he said, "How about a cello concerto?" I immediately thought of John Ehde. That's how it all started. It took them two years to actually produce the commission. I started to compose. At several points Göran phoned me in the hospital and asked how it was going, and I hadn't started. Nothing was going on. I said we'd just have to wait. "That's fine," he said. Another three months he phoned me again. "Nothing's happened," I said. "I'm still very ill. The panic attacks are getting worse." I really felt pressure and thought I was going to fail.

ARAM: How did you actually begin composing, then?

TOMMIE: Near the Naturhistoriska Riksmuseet in Stockholm, there is this bookshop. I was walking with sticks because I couldn't do so otherwise—this was maybe a year after the operation when I woke up with numb legs. This bookshop also sold books on CDs, sounds of rainforests, minerals, fossils, that sort of thing. I saw in the window what I thought was Mahler because it said *Song of Earth*, and I thought, why are they selling Mahler in here? When I looked closer, I saw the CD was recordings by NASA, released by someone named Dr. Jeffrey Thompson.[47] I bought it and put it on one night when I was alone in the house. I had started to write the cello concerto, but I had no idea where to go with it, no idea whatsoever.

Just before that, I'd stayed at a spa for many weeks because of all my pain and panic disorder. I put that CD on, and I felt immediately this low C# and very high D#. Very high and very low. It was this warm sound, these sounds coming at me. And I thought, I absolutely must use this in the cello concerto to open another window, like a window to escape out of this anxiety. I decided the concerto would begin and end with these notes. I thought about how I would do this live, with loudspeakers in the orchestra. I read the liner notes about Dr. Jeffrey Thompson. It looked like you couldn't call Jeffrey Thompson, but you could fax him. I was

47 Dr. Jeffrey Thompson, American electronic composer and researcher into clinical neuroacoustics; creator of numerous CDs of music and sound pulses for sleep and relaxation.

Photo: Elisabet Löfberg Haglund

Dr. Jeffrey Thompson in his studio, Encinitas, California, ca. 2003.

anxious because I didn't want to use the NASA sample without permission and then get fined millions of dollars. And I wanted to be able to work immediately, so I phoned the fax number, and he answered because he happened to be standing there mending the fax in San Diego! He lifted up the receiver. I was really confused, so confused that my first question came out, "I'm sorry, what is the time?" [*Laughs.*] "What?" he said. "Well, I'm calling from Sweden," I said. He said, "Are you calling from Sweden to ask about the time?" "No, I'm a composer," I said. [*Laughs.*] "Oh," he said, "I'm composing a bit myself." So that's how it started. We had a long conversation. I asked him about how the sounds on his CD were made, and he told me they had sped up some of the low notes and lowered the high notes until it sounded exactly like human voices. I asked if it would be possible for me to use this in the concerto. "Oh, no problem," he said. "Use it, use as much as you want. With a few conditions, like you have to print the source in the program that it's NASA who's behind this." And the other condition was that I send him a recording of this cello concerto. "And I have another request," he said. "That you and your wife come visit me in San Diego." So, I said yes to all of them. And we went there, of course, and spent a day with him. "It was extraordinary," he said, "because I never answer the fax machine!"

ARAM: I think I listen to his CDs for completely different reasons than the therapeutic ones he intends, but I like it anyway.

TOMMIE: You know, he had this massage table with a huge resonance box under it, and it massaged your internal organs through the sound of the notes. There are spectacles you put on as well, so you can see colors. It massages intestines and stuff. It really worked. You could feel it! Very West Coast.

ARAM: So, tell me about the connection between the space sounds and the cello concerto.

TOMMIE: It took so much time to be able to comprehend what I felt. I knew I wanted to use the orchestra in a traditional way but not—something with a full orchestra where you could still feel very lonely. How does it feel when you're standing alone in front of something ominous, something frightening, beautiful, unavoidable? Like you do when you're looking at stars in the sky—like I did when I was a child in the hospital. Loneliness. I wanted to propel myself into inner space in a way. Just after that, I was taken to Hultafors Sanatorium to rest, this time for three weeks. It was a home for people with rheumatism, I think. I was lying in a room, only walking out if I had the stamina. And I was dreaming up scores. I had music paper in bed, but the nurses took that away from me.

ARAM: They took it away?

TOMMIE: Yes, they took it away. They thought it was not good for my health. I used to hide it somewhere they couldn't find it. So, at nighttime, I'd compose anyway. It was a long journey, and I learned about my own capacity for persistence. Looking back, I can't believe I felt so strongly about expressing myself when I was so mortally ill and when, at times, I couldn't even hold a pen. I have a memory of doing sketches for the concerto in the hospital, and then when we moved to this house, I finished it and wrote it all out.

But you know, I didn't compose the piece after that sound—the NASA sound. It only determined the first two notes. I composed freely after that. I didn't listen to it. I just remembered the atmosphere. When you hear the sound in concert, when it comes out of the loudspeakers... Erik Wallrup[48]—to whom I dedicated it—said it felt to him like opening a gigantic window to space.

ARAM: The NASA sound was broadcast during the performance?

TOMMIE: Yes, yes. And the drums were inspired by hearing the Ojibwe ceremonial music in Canada. That was such an ecstatic thing, something way above our rational and so-called civilized world. Okko Kamu was the conductor for the premiere. The first

---

48 Erik Wallrup, professor of musicology at Stockholm University and a well-known author and critic in Scandinavia, and one of Haglund's closest confidantes.

performance was pretty rough—not because of John's playing. John's playing was fantastic, in fact. He got out all the emotions he had it seemed. But I felt the conductor didn't make use of all the details I had carefully thought out. I didn't hear it fully realized until the Gothenburg Symphony played it, with all the possibilities and details.

In Gothenburg, in 2012, when they did the cello concerto twice, it transformed between performances. The program was my cello concerto and Shostakovich's Symphony No. 10. There was this young conductor, maybe thirty-two or thirty-three, very gifted, named David Afkham. He's now the principal conductor of the Spanish National Orchestra. The first time, he played it like an ordinary piece. I think, to be safe, he chose a much higher tempo than indicated in the score, and it didn't come out the way I wanted it to. I said, "Listen, you have to pretend that you're much older, with more experience than you have now." "But I'm old enough," he said. "That's not what I mean. You need to have faced death, close into your face. I wish you never will for many years, but you have to pretend that you have. Think about Bruckner," and by that, I meant his manifestation of the absolute, religious ecstasy, and taking time. "And don't listen to the orchestra. Listen to the audience. How long can I remain silent before the next phrase? Listen to them like a stand-up comedian would." I said that to the cellist about the cadenzas as well. If you deliver the punchline one split-second too early, there will be some laughter, but it will be twice as much if you time it perfectly. That's John Cleese's gift—what he taught me.

Ten years later, to my great surprise, the cello concerto received the Christ Johnson Prize for 2014.[49]

ARAM: What do you think inspired it, aside from the circumstances of your life at the time?

TOMMIE: I had some almost hallucinatory experiences, but mostly utter loneliness, like being a voice that no one can ever hear. Those feelings occurred very often when I did that piece. I wasn't listening to much else, certainly no other cello concertos. I did listen to Scelsi while in hospital, particularly *Anahit*. He managed to make music totally out of time, almost like something from before man existed. Or like a soundtrack to the dreams I had of being in underground caves with lions. I had similar feelings while writing the cello concerto. I really wanted to reach into inner space as far as I could.

ARAM: Were you trying to make a total statement? An attempt to say everything at once: an *allkonstverk*?

TOMMIE: Yes, yes. In a way. It's a preparation for death. Though if I was to write a preparation for death now, I would do it differently. But during the period of my life in which I wrote it, that's how I felt. The cello concerto was to be my final statement.

ARAM: I think you've done that more than once! [*Laughs.*]

TOMMIE: [*Laughs.*] Yes, I always have this feeling that what I'm writing might be the last thing I ever write.

ARAM: It's certainly an economical approach—say only what's important enough to survive you after death.

---

49 Christ Johnson Prize, an occasional prize awarded by the Kungliga Musikaliska Akademien (Swedish Academy of Music), is the most prestigious in Scandinavia.

TOMMIE: I was genuinely sure I wasn't going to live very long. By 2005, I'd even made arrangements with the insurance company for my own funeral, got it all paid for, and chose the music.

ARAM: And yet soon after, you composed the piece for flute and percussion, *Varsamt, Victoria sover* [*Gently, Victoria is Sleeping*], which was completed in 2001.

TOMMIE: Yes. I wrote that for my daughter. She's a very gifted painter, but she's now studying medicine. This is Victoria, my first daughter. I remember the night she was born, and I was thinking of that when I was composing *Varsamt*. It was a very difficult birth for Helen. They had to sedate her. So, I took care of Victoria for the first few hours of her life, and we bonded very closely. I promised her I'd never let her down, this little girl, as she held my thumb. When I left the hospital, I took my Volvo PV to the coast, where there is a Stone Age graveyard. It was late at night. The sea was roaring. It was so windy, and a severe storm came up. I just stood there and thought about what my life had become and what my daughter's would be. Then, I went home and lit a candle and listened to Chopin's Piano Concerto No. 1, the slow movement. *Varsamt* is about Victoria dreaming. The thunder from the night she was born is in the background percussion.

ARAM: Who commissioned *Varsamt*?

TOMMIE: [*Pause.*] You know, I don't recollect. Gunilla von Bahr, perhaps. When the musicians were to premiere *Daughter of the Voice* at the St. Birgitta 700th Jubilee in 2003, the percussionist, Markus Leoson, wondered if I had anything for percussion. I said I did and sent him the score for *Varsamt*, but I had no idea they would record it and put it on a CD. No idea whatsoever. I guess he lost one page, or I didn't give it to him, or someone made a mistake somewhere. So, when I got the CD, I thought, oh no, there is something lacking here. Even they thought it was a bit curious—the way it ended. I pointed it out to them. They made it work, but I'd like to have a new recording of that piece.

ARAM: Overlapping this to an extent was work on *Daughter of the Voice*. How did that piece come about?

TOMMIE: Stephan Borgehammar, the guy who represented the Stiftelsen S:Ta Birgittasystrarna[50] had seen me on television in connection with the cello concerto. What happened was that Elisabet and I had gotten married in July of 2000. We had gone to the Swedenborgian Church in Stockholm to see if anyone could marry us, and there we met Rev. Göran Appelgren and his wife, Josephine. After the ceremony, we went to Corsica for our honeymoon. We took a trip on a bus up one thousand meters to a village inhabited only by artists. It's been populated for thousands of years—a very old village, but now it's an artists' colony. We went into this shop where they made music boxes or rather the wooden boxes. Some of them looked dreadful. When we went into the shop, all these machines were playing at once. And I managed to discover one tune. I heard one tune coming through the rest that sounded so beautiful. I managed to get hold of it. I went to the desk—the girl couldn't understand me, of course, but I was asking, what's this song? What's the text about? She said she couldn't explain, but I could take the box across the street to the record shop and ask the man there. So, the man told me it was a sacred text about a donkey

50 Stiftelsen S:Ta Birgittasystrarna, an order of nuns dedicated to St. Bridget.

or something, presumably with Christ. The piece I was writing for St. Birgitta's was about the crucifixion, so this fit perfectly. Just when I was about to pay for the thing, Elisabet came up and said, "Come on, Tommie, you have to go! The bus won't wait! We won't get out of here until tomorrow otherwise." "But I have to pay," I begged. "No, come!" I was in shorts, with one leg twice as thin as the other one, and a Panama hat. I looked stupid, and I was sent onto the bus without the music box. I was devastated. How I wanted to have this machine. I knew I would use it somewhere! We were back at the hotel in Calvi, and I told the hotel manager that I was writing music about a Swedish saint, and he talked to one of his staff members. They actually took a car the whole way up and got the music box for me!

ARAM: How did they know which of all the music boxes in the shop?

TOMMIE: Oh, I told them to explain at the shop what the text was about, and that this strange Swede had been in there and didn't buy it. Imagine if they'd come back with one playing Disney tunes! Anyway, I've got the music box here at home. I had originally considered amplifying the music box itself for *Daughter of the Voice*, but it ended up that I only used the theme.

ARAM: Why did you not amplify the box?

TOMMIE: I don't know. I was first thinking of starting with it, but then, when I was focusing on composing the crucifixion, I was thinking instead, what's the worst thing on earth? I couldn't decide, so I asked, what's the worst thing in music? And that's the metronome. And if you have three metronomes, that's even worse!

Photo: Örjan Henriksson

Tommie Haglund, ca. 1995

If you set them differently, you count different speeds—one to 163, one to 180—all together, they create a certain rhythm.

ARAM: They syncopate?

TOMMIE: They do something you can't do with an instrument. A human can't do it. It's inhuman. It sounds almost like a tango, but also something terrible like driving nails through your hands, lots of nails through lots of hands. That's why I wanted to start like that. I thought that would be more effective than thunder. It did really create an effect in the concert hall when they had these purple lights, almost like Scriabin's *Poeme du feu*, where you have colors in the score. A frightening effect, really. When you buy the score, it comes with a CD with those metronomes recorded.

ARAM: A couple of years later, you went to the United States to give a lecture, and that was the beginning of *Hymnen an die Nacht*.

TOMMIE: Yes, there were so many things happening at that time, and I was so ill. That's when the nightmare really began.

Part Three

INFINITY

16: THE JOURNEY INWARD

Compositions: Hymnen an die Nacht | La Rosa Profunda

ARAM: The violin concerto explores many personal facets, doesn't it? It's much more than a soundtrack to Novalis' poem. It's one of those rare pieces of music that really can't be expressed in any other way but as music. How did you come to create it?

TOMMIE: I was invited to the United States to lecture about my music and prepare for a concert in collaboration with music students at the Juilliard School in New York. After the lecture at the Glencairn Museum, outside Philadelphia, there was a luncheon, and I sat next to a man in his mid-sixties—a rather reserved, almost shy fellow. He told me he had bought a violin for his daughter, a concert violinist. "Interesting," I said. "What sort of violin?" "It's the Red Violin, the one Hollywood made a film about. The legend said that when Stradivarius built it, his wife died in childbirth, and he took a few drops of her blood and put it in the varnish. Hence the name. It disappeared in the nineteenth century and then turned up in an auction in New York, and I bought it for two million dollars for her fifteenth birthday." I was stunned. Who was this? I asked his name. "Laren Pitcairn, my daughter is Elizabeth Pitcairn." "Amazing," I said. "The same name as the man who built the château in Grez-sur-Loing taken care of by Soldanella's father." "Yes," he said. "Theodore Pitcairn was my father. My daughter now lives in Los Angeles, but she's here now and wants to meet you. If you'd like, I could pick you up tomorrow, and you could see where we live."

The next day, he picked me up, and I was taken to their home in Bucks County. I was seated, and after a while, Elizabeth came in with her violin. I could see she was nervous and asked if there was something I wanted to hear. I said, "How about something from Sibelius' Violin Concerto?" She played it effortlessly. Then she played Paganini, Tchaikovsky, and some other things. I was really impressed. We took a walk on the grounds, and she said her family was involved in supporting the arts: the Curtis Institute, the Philadelphia Orchestra, and so on. She asked, would I be interested in a commission for a violin concerto.

"Say a price."

I thought for a while and asked for what I thought was a good payment.

"Fair enough," she said.

After I was home, Elizabeth's mother phoned. We talked for a while, and then she said she wanted to do something pastoral.

Without thinking, I said, "Then it's better that you call a Hollywood composer. I don't take any instructions when I'm to compose."

There was a long silence. And then she said, "I like a man with guts. Do it your way, Tommie."

So, I started, but I had no idea what I was doing.

ARAM: Did you begin with a sound, like you did with *Intensio Animi*, or with a concept?

TOMMIE: Sometimes, I think experience itself is not fulfilled without putting art into it. That's exactly why I'm doing art. I used to think maybe I composed to escape reality, but really, no, I'm trying to get closer to it. Going into myself is the opposite of escape. I'm surprised at what comes out. But why am I doing this? It would be so much easier and more comfortable, so I imagine, to have a regular job and get together with friends for coffee and go to the bar. But I'm so constantly in contact with my inner world, and I sometimes envy the idea of having an ordinary job, but then I know I can't live any other way. I never let it go because I'm afraid it won't come back.

ARAM: The violin concerto is, perhaps, one of the more "contemporary" sounding of your works. But also, one of the most introverted, which makes a lot of sense for a connection with Novalis. Were you reading Novalis at the time?

TOMMIE: No, it was Erik Wallrup who suggested I read it. I have to tell you a little about him. Erik is one of my closest friends. I first met him at Berwaldhallen in Stockholm in 1995, when there was a concert featuring my music. Göran Bergendahl, who was master of ceremonies at the concert, told me a man was sitting, listening intensively at the rehearsals.

"Who was it?" I asked.

"Erik Wallrup, the main critic at the *Svenska Dagbladet*."

He wrote a fantastic review, and we met the day after the concert for coffee. We talked about the possibility of him writing the liner notes for the Caprice CD. We had so much to talk about, and he is a superb writer and scholar in music. He looked like a teenager to me, then. He was the best man at my wedding and I in his. He always puts everything in balance for me. The way he writes about music is beautiful and full of insights.

Anyway, years later, I played some of the chords of the violin concerto I was working on on the piano, and he said it immediately put him in mind of Novalis, saying they were part of the same atmosphere.

ARAM: So, you were actually working on the violin concerto before it became, thematically, *Hymnen an die Nacht*? And Erik Wallrup came along and heard Novalis in it?

TOMMIE: Yes. Erik's doctoral dissertation is about *Stimmung* and Heidegger—a hugely academic and very interesting book. It was when he first heard my work at Berwaldhallen that he decided that, of the arts, music has the greatest possibilities for producing *Stimmung*. The room can vibrate. When I sent him the string trio, he wrote that it stirred up all the sadness in his life and didn't know how to explain it. He sees things that seem to exist below what I'm writing.

ARAM: What was it like composing the violin concerto?

TOMMIE: I wrote *Hymnen an die Nacht* locked in this house because of panic attacks. For one and a half years, I couldn't leave. When I finished, I phoned Daniel Börtz,[51] who said,

"What note did it end with?"

---

51 Daniel Börtz is a Swedish composer who worked with Ingmar Bergman and wrote several symphonies performed in Sweden and abroad.

And I said, "It ended with a C-sharp."

"Oh," he said, "It's a pity you didn't end with a C; then it would be in perfect balance."

He said that as a joke, but I took it seriously anyway. I felt I wasn't really in balance at all. Really dreadful. When I wrote all that music, I really thought I was dying. I was sure. Infections, Penicillin, cramps, fever, panic, blood poisoning. I was at the emergency room once per week. Elisabet was sitting up all night sometimes. When I finished *Hymnen an die Nacht,* I walked down the hill, and suddenly, I couldn't stand, so I had to crawl back up the hill to the house. It took half an hour to go one hundred meters. I didn't say anything to Elisabet about that. The morning after, I wanted to sit by the piano and work, but suddenly, I just couldn't move. I had been to a psychiatrist who told me I had the same disease as Schumann. She told me to read books about Schumann and see how much we're alike. She gave me another book about Mozart. She told me I was able to compose because I had some type of brain—a gift with a price. I accepted that. Elisabet never accepted it. I believed in that for a time. Of course, you can always see what you want to see. The same psychiatrist told me I had epilepsy and I needed electroshock therapy.

ARAM: What??

TOMMIE: So, they gave me that. Four or five times, and I never should have had it.

ARAM: That's for sure!

TOMMIE: So, I was in hospital for five weeks at this psychiatric clinic. Locked in, with electroshock, and thirty tablets a day.

ARAM: How many?!

TOMMIE: I was diagnosed as bipolar. I thought this is the way it is. The medicine made it worse and worse. There was one and a half years when I couldn't go outside these walls. I could go to the beginning of the path, but once I reached there, I had to go back. I often ended up with my friends, saying a sentence, then one minute later repeating myself. I was completely gone. My muscles had collapsed and didn't work. I could only walk with a stick, and I had to wear glasses to see. I was always fighting serious infections. That's why it was life-threatening—I had blood poisoning. Sepsis. They had me on Xanax, Lamictal, Lithium, Propavan, Imovane, and Oxascand—those are the ones I can recollect.

ARAM: I can't believe the cocktail they had you taking. It sounds like they were just throwing everything at you and hoping something would stick.

TOMMIE: At one point, I accidentally took a double dose of one of the medicines because the new tablets looked the same as the old ones. I couldn't even stand up. The walls were spinning upward. I was a pharmaceutical experiment. I just had to lie down and shake and tell Elisabet the notes and values for the *La Rosa Profunda* song cycle.

ARAM: Aside from the fact that Delius was blind, the connection between this and him in his later years is worth pointing out.

TOMMIE: In a way, Elisabet was my Fenby, yes. It was an enormous effort because there were only a couple of weeks before the premiere of *La Rosa Profunda* for a big jubilee in Halmstad [in 2007]. The town was to celebrate 700-*årsjubileum*, and Barbara Bonney was engaged to sing this new work of mine. We talked on the phone several times, and then one day, she sounded incredibly sad. She was to separate from her husband and had no stamina left. Jeanette Köhn sang the work instead.

ARAM: Why did you choose *La Rosa Profunda* for the 700th anniversary concert?

TOMMIE: At the time, I was reading Lewis Carroll's *Through the Looking Glass* and somehow stumbled into Borges and read a poem by him about Swedenborg. All three are talking about an inner world. I didn't really think this would fit a celebration of the anniversary of a town, but I didn't care; I just wanted to represent honestly how I was feeling and how important it is to keep your inner space intact. Well, when they were to rehearse *La Rosa Profunda*, I was too sick to go. I was so ill that I couldn't do anything, really, and it was a miracle I could stand up in the church. I was sweating and pale; that's how it was. I managed to go once to the church to correct Jeanette Köhn's pronunciations. She used to sing for the Nobel Prize ceremony. Love Derwinger, the pianist, has recorded many times for BIS. They were preparing as if for the Olympics, you know, like the way you concentrate before a tennis match or something—very serious. So, it was a concert with Grieg, Clara Schumann, and Fanny Mendelssohn, and they played *Arcana* as well. Great interpretation. And then, at the end, they played *La Rosa Profunda*. The audience must have been really tired, sitting there in the church, but they were so silent. I was, of course, very nervous. And then, in the end, there was this enormous ovation. Standing, whistling, screaming. So here I was, on stage, barely propped up, and an enormous line of people waiting to talk to me. My mother was there, and all she could think was that I was wearing the wrong clothing. I'd borrowed a Chinese jacket from Elisabet's cousin Björn.

ARAM: Was it a Mandarin collar, like Mao's?

TOMMIE: It wasn't at all. It was a very luxurious silk jacket.

17: JOHN CLEESE

ARAM: Do some of your works capture things you consider to be entirely negative, or even represent failures to capture?

TOMMIE: There's one piece in which I tried to capture the complete emptiness when I thought everything was over. It's the trio for clarinet, violin, and piano, *Frammenti,* which is in three movements, each focusing on one note, not like Scelsi, but in a different way. The premiere at the Chamber Music Festival in Båstad turned out well, even though it wasn't really written for people to listen to. I just felt I had to sort myself out and get rid of everything. I really thought my life was over. This was 2008. But that's why I've written so few pieces; it takes so much energy from me. There was another piece, for double bass and cello, *Acedia,* where I do think I failed. The cellist disagreed. He said it was almost sacred to him. [*Laughs.*] But I was simply too ill and mentally confused to do it. It was about my childhood.

ARAM: Who finally got you off all these meds?

TOMMIE: Another doctor came in after a few years and looked at my files and said there was nothing mentally wrong with me. She took me off everything immediately, including the Benzodiazepine. It took one year to taper off it all. We lived one day at a time, Elisabet and I. We didn't know what would happen. Some friends who paid us a visit at that time left and said to each other, he's dying. But then, once I stopped all the medications, after a few weeks, I had no stick, no glasses, and no infections. I lost many years. I did compose, but . . .

ARAM: What's so unbelievable is how unnecessary much of it was. There must have been a sense of relief as the effects began to subside.

TOMMIE: I felt an immense happiness. The *Hymnen an die Nacht* CD came out at just this time, 2010, and there was a Grammy nomination, and all these positive reviews were coming out of England and everywhere, even Poland. Prizes and money were coming my way. It all started happening at the same time. I was celebrating, and I couldn't believe it had all happened under those circumstances.

ARAM: Or because of them.

TOMMIE: I really didn't know what to do with myself. I thought for a while, well, I could just lean back and be done with these things, and it'll be fine, but what am I going to do? I can't do anything else, really, but write music.

ARAM: I saw images of Donald Duck and Laurel and Hardy in the upstairs sitting room. I wondered whether they represent something innocent to you, something antithetical or antidotal to the angst you have said you feel.

TOMMIE: Oh yes. Absolutely. There is innocence there, in a way, and it's important to me. Every day, on one of the channels, there was an hour of Laurel and Hardy. I never missed it. I lived for it. That sort of naïve humor is so childish, but it's good. I was laughing and every day looking forward to the next day. It was the same thing with *Fawlty Towers* and *Monty Python*—they meant so much to me. And I thought, I have to thank John Cleese. I felt some percentage of my success with *Hymnen an die Nacht* belonged to John Cleese. But he is known for saying no to everything—interviews, meetings, and so on. I found an email address for his agent, but I thought, if I write and say I'm a composer and I want to thank John Cleese, they will never answer. I somehow found a phone number for his agent's wife—I don't recollect her name. I thought if he says no, that's fine. So, I phoned and explained who I was, and she said, "We've heard something about a violin and *Fawlty Towers*, is that you?" I didn't know what she meant, so I just said something, and she replied, "My husband will call you." I thought he never would. But he did.

ARAM: Did he?

TOMMIE: Yes, he did. It turned out John was to come to Sweden as part of a comedy tour. I believe it was the Alimony Tour. He's actually very difficult to meet. His agent said it was easier to meet Obama than John Cleese. Anyway, we went to Jönköping, where he was to perform. It was packed with people, of course. We were to see him after the performance, so we went up on stage and met his agent. Elisabet and Sven were there with me. I hadn't mentioned it, but I thought if anyone is to meet Cleese, it should be Sven. And you know, Cleese is six-five, but Sven is nearly six-seven

Photo: Elisabet Löfberg Haglund

Tommie Haglund with John Cleese, 2010

and is a kind of Clint Eastwood type. The first thing Cleese asked was, "Who's he?" And my reply was, "Well, this is our daughter." [*Laughs.*]

ARAM: [*Laughs.*]

TOMMIE: Cleese laughed, of course, and he also made a joke about Elisabet's British accent, but I could also tell he wanted to be serious. I told him the story of the illness, and he listened very intently. I told him I thought his comedy had saved me, saved my life, in a way. I made sure he realized I wasn't saying he, John Cleese, had saved me, but rather his comedy had. That's too big a responsibility to put on someone. When I signed the CD for him, I wrote,

"I think you're the Beethoven of comedy." I told him about writing the violin concerto and how *Fawlty Towers* had really helped me and Elizabeth Pitcairn get through the difficulties of interpreting and recording it. There were times when she would spend the whole day building and building toward a very serious performance, but in order to release the tension, we had to then go straight in the opposite direction—so we watched *Fawlty Towers,* and she'd go back downstairs and nail the movements. I've never seen someone laugh as hard as she did. John's comedy really allowed me to carry on through a horrendous time. He wanted to know about Elizabeth Pitcairn's violin. He asked, "Are they the ones who own the Pitcairn Islands?" "Maybe," I said, "I don't know!" I said to him, "After years of being severely medicated, I don't know who I am anymore. And I don't know how to write, don't know what to write about, and I'm afraid of opening the gates of anxiety again." I hadn't written anything for a year by that time because I was afraid of the anxiety.

ARAM: Right.

TOMMIE: We talked a lot about creativity and how difficult it had been for me to compose recently. So, Cleese said, "If you can, try giving lectures about creativity. That's what I've been doing. For businesspeople, mainly. Talk about yourself and your music and play extracts of your music from CD, and it'll come back." I thought that was a very good suggestion. You can think back inside yourself, and think back, and think back, and you go nowhere, but when you tell it to someone and get reactions, something begins to happen. He said he was Europe's most unmusical man, but I told him, "I know that's not true," because then he wouldn't have the perfect timing he has. We parted ways, and as I was walking out, he said, "Please stop, come back." And suddenly, he grabbed me and just held me—remember, he's six feet, five inches, and I still had a cane, I think. It must have looked really strange. He said, "I promise I'll listen to your CD tonight when I get to the hotel, and I'll tell you what I think. Promise me one thing," he said—and I think we both had tears in our eyes—"promise that you'll take care of yourself. God bless you."

On our way home, John's agent phoned to thank us and say that John had been so moved and that it had been one of the most interesting meetings he'd had in a long time. Later, I heard from him about how much he liked the violin concerto. He is a very kind, almost fatherly figure. I felt as if I had given him something, at least. I really hate name-dropping and trading on other people—it's unjust to them—but I keep that meeting in here [*points to his heart*]. To be able to say how much he meant to me was the crowning of all those years of pain. It was also an incredible meeting, in a way—such a contrast. [*Laughs.*] Later, I heard how interested he had become in Bergman, Strindberg, and so on. The seriousness of the Scandinavian artists! Even he! I think his search for the important things in life, not just jokes, has made him one of the funniest people on the planet.

ARAM: Did you give those lectures on creativity, as he suggested?

TOMMIE: I did, and it really helped. I had conversations with my friend Bengt Johnsson here in Halmstad, who had good connections with businesspeople. He arranged a lecture for CEO types in the western part of Sweden. Then, it kept going. I soon realized that it could take over everything.

One afternoon, I was sitting with Bo Strömberg at Regnbågen. We were talking about all this and how much there was to do. Then, he said a thing that upset me but woke me up: "Why are you doing this when you are supposed to write music?" Only someone who knows you and wants the best for you would say that. It was then that I decided to sharpen up and go back to composition only.

ARAM: I'm interested in the fact that comedy was so important to you at a time you were writing music that, I think I can say, demands to be taken very seriously.

TOMMIE: Someone asked me why I don't put any humor in the music. I never felt the need, really, like Shostakovich, doing humoristic, ironic pieces—cartoon music.

ARAM: There is the risk of one-dimensionality. And it's not as if there's no humor possible in the music, just no comedy. The stamp of your personality on the music wouldn't be complete without some kind of built-in relief from the seriousness of the subject matter. It's there—humor—otherwise, paradoxically, I don't think anyone would take your music seriously.

TOMMIE: That's right, I hope. In *Intensio Animi* there are parts in which I send the cellist straight into madness. What I have avoided—and this I see as a weakness, in a sense—is comedy. Laughter. I was interviewed on a television program many years ago, and they asked if I would ever write Donald Duck music. You know, something humorous as a contrast to everything else I do. Humor is another thing to me. The clowning, that's another world.

18: SOLACE AFTER THE STORM

Compositions: Sollievo dopo la tempesta | Serenata per Diotima | Di sogno tessuto

ARAM: Tell me about the string trio, *Sollievo dopo la tempesta [Solace after the storm]*.

TOMMIE: That piece I began composing about a year after I freed myself from all the medications.

ARAM: So, this was beginning in 2012?

TOMMIE: Yes. My violin concerto was Grammy-nominated, and I met Cecilia Zilliacus[52] at the ceremony. Actually, it was at the party afterward. We sat at the same table. Caprice Records did a recording of the Bach *Goldberg Variations*—I believe it was even their final recording. They were a state-financed label, and I think the government decided to shut everything down—lots of things were shut down—so Caprice went into the grave. Anyway, they

---

52 Cecilia Zilliacus (1972–) is a Finnish-Swedish violinist and associate professor at the Royal College of Music in Stockholm.

received a Grammy for that *Goldberg Variations* record, and that's why I ended up sitting with Cecilia Zilliacus at the dinner table. And she asked whether I could write a trio for them, ZPR, which is Zilliacus-Persson-Raitinen. They had applied for money from the Kulturrådet,[53] I believe. When I went back home, I thought, well, you must be in a life's crisis if you're going to write a string trio.

ARAM: [*Laughs.*] Why particularly a string trio? Why is that particularly crisis-induced?

TOMMIE: It's particularly difficult to make a string trio . . . effective. And you really are revealed in the most painful ways. A string trio, there's certainly a lot you can do, but it's also limited . . . so limited and yet so unlimited, as I found out.

ARAM: Limited, meaning you have so little to hide behind? But also, so much to account for?

TOMMIE: Yes, that's it. I really went through hell before I could find out what I was going to do. I studied a lot of the old trios. Beethoven, and also Henze's string trios, and Schnittke. I actually ended up listening to Armenian folk music.

ARAM: Oh really? Which songs?

TOMMIE: It was a Jordi Savall recording. I started listening to that, and I found the scales reminded me of Scandinavian folk music. If you listen to the beginning of the string trio, it's the first time I approached folk music. I don't think I was conscious of it, but I really got some inspiration from that old Armenian music. I started with that, but I couldn't find my way. I stopped and started again, stopped and started again, but I couldn't find a

53 Kulturrådet, Swedish Arts Council.

way to continue. Then, I began thinking about Schubert. I don't know why Schubert came into my mind, but I started mixing that into the music, and the old anxiety returned. I tried to manage it by coming back to this folk music. I phoned Cecilia Zilliacus, and they wanted it immediately, but I said I haven't got it yet, wait another year. I tried again. I simply couldn't do it. I tried and tried before I managed to put the thing together.

I was so critical, and I felt so much doubt about what I was doing. I didn't want to go back to writing purely tonal music. I was finding something in major chords, but without being banal. I thought I was on the edge of being banal, really, but Erik Wallrup was here one summer evening and said he wanted to listen to some parts of it. And I thought, he'll just smash this to pieces. He'll say it's rubbish. On the contrary, he was quite the opposite. So, I went on, and I did it. That was the first piece I actually got through after the medication.

ARAM: What did you think of it?

TOMMIE: I didn't know what to think about it. It moved Elisabet to tears when I played it on the piano. As I said earlier, in a crisis I always turn to Dowland. No quotations, like in the violin concerto, but echoes of his melancholic approach. And phrasings that glance at the music of Victoria.

In the autumn of 2013, we went up to Stockholm for the premiere at the concert house. Anders Hallengren[54] was there. I didn't have a title yet. He was listening to the rehearsal during the daytime.

---

54 Anders Hallengren (1950–2024) was a Swedish scholar and author, several of whose works are related to Swedenborg.

He came with his daughters. I said, "I can't find a title." He replied, "There's something healing in the music for me. *Sollievo*." "What?" I said. "*Sollievo*." "OK, *Sollievo*." *Sollievo dopo la tempesta*—so I took that and put it in the program. They introduced it that way. But before they played it, they had this strange arrangement by an operetta singer; it was part-musical and part-opera, or maybe not part-musical but trying to mix hard rock with classical musicians and a singer who used to do musicals. I tried but did not understand the mixture. And you know, musicals—they are not my favorite.

ARAM: Mine neither.

TOMMIE: And they had this rock n' roll accompaniment. And they did that before the string trio. The way all the elements worked together . . . well, they didn't work together—with all respect. But anyway, they did that. The next morning in the paper, a reviewer had the same impression of it that I did.

ARAM: For whom did you write the trio?

TOMMIE: I wrote that trio to thank Ann Marie Belfrage—she was the managing director of Phono Suecia, which is the label that helped launch so many of the contemporary Swedish composers. She told me about the emotional experience she had recording *Hymnen an die Nacht*, and we became close friends after that. She was an immense support while I was ill. She called me when it had been recorded and asked what was behind this painful record. I often felt that she reminded me of Soldanella with her aristocratic elegance and humor. I wrote the string trio partly to thank her, and there are hints of the Swedish folk song "Jag vet en dejlig rosa" ["I Know a Lovely Rose"]. In the introduction, I used the notes

B – E – La – F – D (for R) – A – G – E. No one knew that then except Ann Marie.

ARAM: Until now. [*Laughs.*] What do you think is behind it? What does it express?

TOMMIE: Healing after a very long period of suffering. What was left, and what I thought must be transformed, was sadness. I found it will always remain. But in order to have the strength to go on, my perception must change. The solution wasn't groping in the dark, and it risks banality. Pain is inevitable. *Sollievo* doesn't mean I'm using anesthesia over myself. It's about turning away from the bitterness that might have dominated my life. There's a certain resignation that comes with age, and you can hear it, I hope, at the end of the piece—a desolation that sometimes crops up in my inner being when sadness refuses to let go.

ARAM: I think I understand.

TOMMIE: There's a lot of regret and a lot of sadness in the music. And anxiety. It ends with a cleansing.

ARAM: The music itself can affect a kind of cleansing?

TOMMIE: I don't know. Perhaps it feels like that of the relation to Renaissance music and Dowland. What do you think?

ARAM: I think relief can be felt, but I don't know about cleansing. Relief is also such an easy thing to affect in music. You just have to push the limits of what's tolerable and then pull back to allow a sense of relief from it. All pleasure is relief—isn't that what a famous junkie once said?[55]

---

55 The "famous junkie" is William S. Burroughs.

TOMMIE: I think I'm approaching tonality in a way that I haven't dared do before. Maybe that's what I'm talking about. It wasn't the right time for that until the string trio.

ARAM: What was it about that point in time that felt right for expansion into tonality?

TOMMIE: To me, the chords in the string trio are more otherworldly, more open, and that lends itself to tonal progression.

ARAM: Interesting. I would think dream logic would exceed tonal progression right away.

TOMMIE: It's not tonal progression with a dominant and a sub-dominant. I mean, there's a tonal center like in Scelsi, where there's a central note. I think of the tonalities as more like shifts in color with a solid ground to stand on, not a progression in the formal sense.

ARAM: Speaking of tonality, tell me about *Serenata per Diotima*. It's different from the pieces of that era.

TOMMIE: That was commissioned by the Kulturskolan through the headmaster there, Ulf Fembro. He was the former theater director of Tornedalsteatern and worked with many famous playwrights and later applied for the job of director at the Kulturskolan here in Halmstad. He suggested to the head string teacher, Mats Reuter, that they commission something for me. So, they asked if I'd write something for sixty string players or something, students and former students at the cultural center.

ARAM: [*Laughs.*]

TOMMIE: And I thought, how am I going to do that? I'll have to control myself and not write passages that are too difficult for them to play. And then my granddaughter was born. I remember when I first saw her and looked into her eyes. She's got very strong eyes, that girl. I thought the thing to do as I write this piece is to think of her and nothing else. Let go of all the anxiety and all the old influences. See if I can think only of this girl. Let it end in peace. There are gestures to Delius and Mahler and Bruckner, of course, but the piece is a tribute to my granddaughter. I phoned Mats Reuter and asked him if he thought I was on the right track. He was very encouraging. I kept on with it and finished it, and at the rehearsal, the students seemed to be getting it, even though they were chords they'd never played before. It was a good performance. So, that summer, I was to travel to Luzerne, the music camp run by Elizabeth Pitcairn in New York State. They played it there, and it went well again. Before that, I expanded the piece more for professional orchestras. Joachim took it, and we did a recording for BIS with the Malmö Symphony Orchestra and the Bogotá Filharmónica. Erik Wallrup said he thought it was a sign I was going off-track, but the audience in Bogotá gave it a standing ovation in the middle of the concert. [*Laughs.*]

ARAM: Did Erik really say that?

TOMMIE: At first, he wasn't enthusiastic. He said, "If critics now raise you up to the sky based on this piece, are you ready to meet their expectations in the future?" In other words, if I wasn't careful, I could be seduced into writing crowd-pleasers. I told Erik, no, I won't be in prison and won't limit myself to any one thing. But one student I played it for responded by saying it was like telling my granddaughter her whole life. I liked that.

ARAM: Last summer, right here in this room, I watched someone quite overcome by emotion while listening to that piece. You

Photo: Eva Winiarski

Tommie Haglund and the Royal Stockholm Philharmonic Orchestra with conductor Tobias Ringborg. Composer Weekend March 28-31 2019, Stockholm Concert Hall.

know who I'm talking about. Someone I might have thought could only be reached by Yngwie Malmsteen, and yet, there he was crying as the piece went on. He couldn't speak.

TOMMIE: I'd forgotten about that, but you're right. That person asked me afterward, "Have you ever been in a car crash?" I said yes. Helen and I were coming home one January—Amanda was to be born a few months later, so it was 1988. We'd been driving for one and a half hours, and it was dark. It was below zero. I was going too fast, and the car started gliding across the road, and I knew we were going to crash. I thought we would crash into the trees and I'd break my back, but the car turned over into a pond. All the windows smashed, and the doors somehow came open. We would have drowned otherwise. We managed to get out, but it was freezing cold water. We struggled back to the motorway, and there was a truck driver who had stopped and was phoning the police. He drove us to the hospital. None of us were hurt. But the reason this man, who wept after listening to the serenade, asked me that question is because he'd been through a car crash himself.

ARAM: Tell me about *Di sogno tessuto*.

TOMMIE: Well, Anders Wilhelmsson, the organist, phoned me just as I was leaving for Luzerne, which, as I mentioned, is the summer music camp run by Elizabeth Pitcairn. This was 2014, I believe. There is a church organ façade built in the 1940s by a Swedish architect named Ivar Tengbom. It was built during the war, and the sound is very somber. It was made of very cheap material because of wartime rationing. In the 1990s, an organist here had the idea to remove that organ and the façade and build new ones. A Dutch organ builder came and built a new organ and an entirely new façade as well—a big white organ. The old one they just removed. But the local historical preservationist reacted. And there was quite a fuss, really, between the preservation authorities and the organist, who was one of Anders's predecessors. They wrote letters, it was in the newspapers, because the organ was removed without consultation, and so on. So, the new organ remained, but they actually had to put the old façade back! At this time, the old organist had left, and Anders had arrived.

This takes us back to his phone call to me. He said there was to be an opening for the archbishop. Lots of dignitaries would be visiting as well. He said they just wanted a five-minute piece to showcase the organ. And I said I'd do it, but then I forgot about it. I went to Luzerne and forgot all about it. This organ piece was to be premiered in, I think, March of 2015. It was just before Christmas when Anders phoned again and wondered if I had anything ready. And I thought, oh no, I haven't done a thing. He wanted to meet in three days! So, I pulled myself together and wrote four or five pages. I went up to the church at 10 o'clock in the evening. It was maybe two or three days before Christmas Eve. And luckily, he was moved by the work enough to accept it. I told him it wasn't yet finished, and it ended up being not what he asked for at all—not a five-minute organ demo, but a twenty-minute slow-moving piece.

I watched Anders play the piece again and again as the days went along—he even wept a little once as he played—and that affected how I'd go home and continue composing. So, in a sense, the piece was written specifically for him. It was an interesting process.

ARAM: You're not saying that you adapted improvisations made by Anders into the composition, right? You're just saying you may have moved the composition in certain directions having watched him play it.

TOMMIE: No, no, no, you're right. He came to lunch after the demo, and I learned he'd been through a life crisis. The more I got to know him, the easier it became to write for him. He has an enormous emotional register and access to feelings. At one place in the organ piece, there is a great crescendo, and he asked if it would be alright if he screamed right out, and I said yes. It turned into an unexpected, almost frightening effect.

He played it again recently at the Haglund Festival, and now that he knows it so well, he has the freedom to make it his own, which is what I wanted.

ARAM: I'm getting the impression there was a lot of uncertainty in the composition, but that doesn't come across in the piece, at least to me.

TOMMIE: No, I felt much more secure after having written the string trio and the serenade. I felt that I had overcome a lot of my old limitations. I felt much freer, a new kind of freedom. It's like an odyssey of music history, in a way, that piece. You can hear so many periods in it. Baroque, classical, romantic, and very modern. And I think Anders is playing it so well. At one point, I thought of orchestrating it. I think that could be done.

ARAM: What does the phrase *Di sogno tessuto* mean to you?

TOMMIE: The title in Italian means "woven in dreams." It is, in a way, from Shakespeare. Our lives are woven in dreams.

ARAM: Is that from *The Tempest*?

TOMMIE: Yes. It was Elisabet's idea! For the premiere, I saw this new façade for the organ. I thought about how they had this dream about a new organ façade but one that will remain in a dream. That's why I chose the title. There's another layer to it as well, but it pertains to Anders' personal life.

ARAM: You're working on a new symphony this year, to be premiered sometime in 2019. You mentioned it would be dedicated to Claes-Göran Bjerding. Is that because of his presence in the music, or simply because he died a few years ago?

TOMMIE: It's dedicated to Claes-Göran and Erik Fenby. They were my teachers, and I don't know what would have happened if I'd never met them.

ARAM: Why this particular symphony, though?

TOMMIE: I still don't know what direction the music is going to take. There are dark moments coming in. I can feel that already. I'm not fighting it. But I still have the feeling this symphony might be lighter—not lightweight, but in a stronger light than before. If I succeed, the composition will be much richer, and hell will break loose sometimes. Later in his life, Claes-Göran told me he had panic attacks—there, we, and everyone who has gone through something similar, meet. Maybe it sounds strange to salute him this way, but I will not have any jazz trumpet or anything like that! In the end, there's a lonesome trumpet. That's my way of waving to someone who has been invaluable to me and so many of his students.

19: CREATIVITY

ARAM: How do you see yourself in the music? What kind of self-image forms? Something gentle? Something monstrous?

TOMMIE: As long as I can remember, I've been good at getting into states where time disappears. All things are there in the music. When it gets violent, I can feel my father's violence flowing through me. It really resonates with my own anger and pain and frustration, but it feels generational. If I'm convinced that I'm right, I can be so uncompromising. That's not a good thing to be. The older I get, the more I understand the weight of not losing the innocence of discovery. I can glimpse innocent times and unbroken moments of happiness as a child with my grandparents in my own work. It's not about sentimentality but rather allowing space for the things that have been life-preserving. It's so easy to get stuck in what's been miserable. Family life affects my creativity. Other parts, I don't understand myself. Illogical, but they just have to be there. I just let them go, and maybe I will understand one day. We always search, and the more we think we know, the more we realize otherwise. When I'm composing and forget time, I feel like I'm in contact with something greater than myself. Then, I'm a child again. Right now, I want to express love. When I listen back to my own music, it feels like a counterpoint between different feelings. I have to have access to all these feelings within me in order to compose. It's important to go to the limits in both directions, the Apollonian and the Dionysian.

ARAM: How do you reach these states?

TOMMIE: I've been working on my symphony these past weeks, and just today, I had this very scary experience. Elisabet, as you know, went to Stockholm at 6 o'clock this morning. The first thing I did when I woke up was start working on my symphony, before you woke up. After a few minutes, it was like something went through me. Something exterior that ran right through me. I tried to scribble down what I was hearing, but it was too overwhelming. There was so much music coming at me. There were parts I composed six months ago, stored only in my memory, and suddenly, they were there, in front of me, in my mind. I walked out after that was over and started to think: all the conditions under which I've written the music, if you think about the conditions, a sane person wouldn't do that—wouldn't put the effort into it. Being almost unable to hold a pen, trembling from the medicine. But still, I felt even when I was nine years old that I must compose. I never, never doubted that. But on the other hand, I never believed until recently that I would end up being a professional composer.

ARAM: Can anyone learn to work like this?

TOMMIE: So much is about discipline and not giving up until you come as close as possible to what you want to say. I saw an interview with Nigel North, the lutenist. They asked him why he played the lute. He said it's so difficult to play. It's quiet, but every little error is revealed. Each tiny fault you commit with your fingers makes an enormous response. It's so revealing. And he said that he thought it was in his destiny to play that instrument, and that he wished he could tell all his students that if you practice enough and work hard and so on, you'll be a great lutenist. But he couldn't tell them that. There are things you actually can't learn. So, I wonder if Nigel North isn't right, that there are some things you are just born to do.

ARAM: Do you believe that?

TOMMIE: When writing music, I don't force it. When I don't even think I'm composing, that's when the best music comes out. Sometimes, I try not to think of anything. And yet I wonder, why am I doing this? I wasn't born into a musical family. I didn't have any support. I cut my teeth on an instrument I no longer use. Recently, at this festival where they played ten or eleven of my pieces all at once, it struck me: why am I doing this? Me, as a person, I'm a very small thing in all this. I'm very insignificant, actually. You can't learn your own language from someone else. I'm only now beginning to realize that I am a composer. I'm so extremely grateful.

ARAM: I think that's very well described, but how do you see yourself—in what form do you appear in the music itself? If you are a caricature in the creative process, what do you look like?

TOMMIE: I would see myself as a column of fire, sometimes lively with a strong heat, sometimes almost extinguished.

Even if I wanted to write music that was less abstract, there is still a sting of pain. I'm not someone out taking a calm walk. That's not the self I see in the music. I'm the one who needs to concentrate so hard that the heart almost breaks. There are so many aspects of life that yield very strong emotions—strong senses of love and passions that are just as strong as the worst anxieties.

ARAM: You mentioned desperation. You have certainly felt impending doom for your own body or spirit, but what about for the whole world and universe?

TOMMIE: I have, in periods. A few moments every day when I am low. When I'm very depressed, I feel as if everything is a waste of time. Who cares? Why am I composing if not for eternity? So much fantastic music has been written before. Why should I come up with these futile little things? It makes me very heavy in my entire being when I think that the earth will vanish one day, the entire universe. At least, that's what the scientists say. And then I wonder what will happen in the spiritual world if it exists. Will that also go to extinction? That comes to my mind very often. And what will happen if there is an interior extinction as well? I'm supposed to be an intellectual, at least in one sense. And believing in an afterlife, especially in Europe, you're almost considered stupid, an outcast. But I can't help feeling consternated by that thought. There might be something after the body has given up. When you're in—how shall I put it—in the mental condition of feeling you're doing something you love to eternity, and yet this might be extinguished as well.

ARAM: You said you think about these things every day, every week, still?

TOMMIE: I certainly do, but now I'm calmer in the face of things I can't change. But when I was seven, eight, nine, I would lay awake in deep anxiety of the feeling of extinction. I wondered, why am I born if I have to die, having a taste of life, knowing what it means?

ARAM: Do these feelings drive composition?

TOMMIE: I contain those feelings in the compositions. They are all the feelings and anxieties I face but can't otherwise articulate. What I cannot talk about or explain, I have to make music of. When I compose, I enter a state where I can just scream everything out. I look for the most painful things and really get to them. It's like digging into a wound, and suddenly, it doesn't hurt anymore. But it's not really like that anymore.

ARAM: Do you reach culs-de-sac in your own musical logic?

TOMMIE: I sometimes do. Mostly when I'm tired and impatient.

ARAM: Is it your impulse to back out or break through?

TOMMIE: Break through. I sometimes just drop it and do something else—take Sven for a pizza or something; watch *Monty Python*; read Carl Barks's *Adventures of Donald Duck*, Swedenborg, or some fiery book of poetry. An interesting thing, I met this fellow Frank Oteri, who works with the American Composers Society. He's done some electronic music, very hardline modernistic stuff. The director of Boosey & Hawkes took us out for dinner one night in New York, and this Frank Oteri had listened to my music. I asked him whether I would be considered very old-fashioned in his circles, and he said, no, not at all! Those days are gone. Everything's been done in the sense of creating sensation.

ARAM: Has it, though?

TOMMIE: Well, in the sense that you have had chainsaws through the grand piano, it's been done once, and you can't do it twice.

ARAM: What, then, are we coming to? You can never actually go backward. What's emerging? And what's your part in it?

TOMMIE: Yes, what's emerging? I don't know. It feels too pretentious to talk about my part because I'm only one who is creating. I had a student who studied composition at the Royal Swedish Academy of Music in Stockholm—a woman in her thirties. She expressed that she learned something from me in a single lesson that no one had taught her in five years at the Academy because they're all locked up in modernism. "What I'm looking for now," she said, and I agree, "is the major chord." Not the minor chord, the major chord. I've worked a lot in minor chords as codes, minor thirds, and so on in my music. I'm not an anti-modernist. But I'm primarily searching for a new way to approach tonality combined with total chromaticism.

What we in the Western world call tonality has taken a long time to develop. I guess, for a period, we had to free ourselves from major and minor. Schönberg took this on and managed to make music with a completely different toolbox. But to do this, you have to be able to draw a perfect circle—controlling all the rules and knowing them before you can break them down. In his book *Harmonielehre*—a book of five hundred pages—he describes musical development as an orderly, natural process. And it makes me think of the systematicity of Spinoza or Einstein's notion that the simplest way to explain things is the truth—something that would never appeal to some of the so-called postmodernists. I agree we can't go "back" to tonality, so what can we do? I'll never write a sonata in F major [*laughs*]. But are you free only because you avoid major and minor when it's impregnated in the human experience?

ARAM: Do you want to be totally free?

TOMMIE: Free to express the things I need to say, yes. Freedom can be so many things, and that's not always positive. Without rules, no freedom. I have no script when I start composing. I have no idea what will come out. But I know my harmony and counterpoint, and they're present in my subconscious.

ARAM: It seems to me there's both an interest in defining quality in art and a reluctance to think quality is anything but a personal persuasion. We all say things are great, and things are terrible and yet we don't just mean to ourselves. What do we mean?

TOMMIE: That's true. I've met many musicians who are more focused on their technique than creating something that stirs you—you know, being true to the really difficult parts of Paganini. It's much more rewarding to hear a musician who risks his life almost for a phrase. Julian Bream, for instance, constantly puts himself in danger when he's playing.

Quality doesn't have to be complexity. I can be touched to tears by a single melody, even a pop song, at just the right moment, hitting me when I'm most receptive to it. Just at that moment it hits me as strongly as any Bach or Beethoven piece or Dowland. The tune may be extremely simple, two or three chords, but there is something connecting the performance with the music itself. You might have the same song performed by someone else, and it doesn't touch you at all—a piece of music played by someone who doesn't feel it. You heard my string trio, for instance. The first performance, the one they recorded, the one you heard, was good enough. Many people thought it was good enough. And now, when you hear the second recording, they're bringing out all the details and discovering new things to bring out on their own. They're being really careful with every moment of the music. When I compose, I want to be as thoughtful as I can about every phrase. It's rewarding to work with musicians who haven't got a clue what to do with one of my compositions at first. You start working with them, opening up phrases, and then you tell them, now it's your turn. Do whatever you want with the music. If you want to wait here, or you want to push forward, do it. Play it as if you composed it yourself. When you reach that stage with someone, it's the most rewarding. So much of music is like "special effects" in the movies, and I hope I succeed in getting beyond that. Freedom, stepping outside of what's written—that's one kind of quality, I think, when you can do that. It's just as much the performer as the music I write. Bach is so robust that you can sit there and play metronomically, and the music still works—that's quality, too. But both robust and fragile can be quality. On the other hand, Bruckner's work is extremely sensitive, and every moment has to be treated with the utmost care.

ARAM: Is there anything, then, that all music of quality has in common?

TOMMIE: I've thought a lot about that. I had a very interesting comment at a lecture from an elderly woman who never listened to contemporary music at all, really. She'd never heard it—or rather, never listened. I had played the ending of the violin concerto, the most aggressive parts—how I felt when writing the music. I said to the audience, "Can you imagine how you would feel when hearing this inside of you?" She came up to me afterward and said, "That opened up the music completely, and I heard it in a way I would never have otherwise heard it. I experienced things when hearing it that I hadn't done before." This is someone who mainly listened to big band jazz, you know, Duke Ellington. So, hearing this, it's a completely different thing. She said, "If I heard your music on the radio without knowing what it was, I'd turn it off. But now that you told me that this is how *you* felt, *I* felt the most painful things going through my body, but it felt so beautiful at the same time." It changed her perspective on what she considers quality, I think.

I listened to Status Quo the other day—a recent live performance of one of their songs. I liked their energy when I was fifteen or sixteen. The tune is extremely simple, but the energy they put into it was incredible, really vibrant. But after a while I get tired of the music because I want more of other things than just swinging energy. You can't live like that all the time, but sometimes I like it.

ARAM: What's an example?

TOMMIE: Well, sometimes you can hear a blues guitarist, for example, who hasn't got any technique, but when he's playing, he creates this incredible atmosphere. One or two phrases says more than twenty minutes of dazzling classical virtuosity. So, there's quality in one sense—Buddy Guy.

ARAM: Buddy Guy can play!

TOMMIE: But he hasn't got the best of techniques. You have a guitarist like Julian Bream for instance, who is not the best in the world in a technical sense . . .

ARAM: Really?

TOMMIE: No, no! His technique is unreliable! And he knows it. Periodically he had to fight for every note. He told me this himself. But he's such a genius that he can sound unlimited. I've been to concerts of his that were total disasters—didn't justify him as a musician—but other times he'd produce a single phrase that you will remember for a lifetime because it's so beautiful for having the whole spectra of human emotions in it. He's self-taught, largely self-taught. He's a musical demigod to me in one sense. I do think he's the greatest guitarist that ever lived. His understanding of music from the 1500s to Henze—few have such a wide understanding. There's a program now on Swedish television about the making of a hit—all these groups that generated just one hit and never came back. So, quality, or just good luck, or whatever.

ARAM: Borel's Infinite Monkey Theorem.[56]

TOMMIE: That's how I felt at first when my piece *Intensio Animi* was, from my standpoint, a huge success. I wondered if it would be the same thing for me: here today, gone tomorrow. It's a strange thing, quality. I think when you meet people who really love what they do, they are closer to quality, maybe, than those who are playing with a very cynical attitude. I think sometimes Frank Zappa could be very cynical. He was on level with Boulez. It's almost as if Zappa has a real contempt for his audience. But he's still regarded very highly as a composer and musician. And in a sense, he is.

---

56 French mathematician Émile Borel's Infinite Monkey Theorem states that a monkey hitting keys at random on a typewriter keyboard for an infinite amount of time would eventually result in an inadvertently coherent text, such as the complete plays of William Shakespeare.

ARAM: It's almost as if he was composing tongue-in-cheek.

TOMMIE: When I started composing seriously, I often wondered what people were thinking. Sometimes, a musician you regard very highly says, "What you are doing is fantastic, this is really a work of genius," and you don't believe it—you can't. It took a really long time for me to start looking at what I was doing as even worthwhile—that it would be worth anything. When you have people playing your music and saying these flattering things to you or writing to you, you begin to wonder whether maybe there is some quality in the music despite all the doubts you have.

Since I'm working so much with emotions, I find I have to be careful how I explain them verbally. The emotion is a part of the composition. It's never purely cerebral, at least for me. Bach can be highly cerebral. You play the fugue, and it never fails. If you're going to perform a play about a conflict between two people, you have to learn all the nuances in the dialogue and what is expressed between the words. It's not just a matter of reading out the lines.

ARAM: Are you making an analogy between musicians who focus too much on the exactness of their playing and actors who focus too much on their diction, as opposed to the emotion?

TOMMIE: Yes, it depends so much on the performers.

ARAM: What you've laid out is a theory about the relationship between composer and performer. How does this work when the composer and the performer are the same person? Where does the theory go? How, for example, do you make distinctions among improvised pieces? Or compositions that involve chance procedures?

TOMMIE: I've used improvisation in two or three compositions. In the cello concerto, there's a part where the NASA sound comes in, where the cello sets free. If the cellist is unsure, I do provide some clues, but otherwise, it's up to him or her what to play. You really need a confident performer for that. Many classical musicians aren't used to improvisation. They were in the nineteenth century, eighteenth century. Take Mozart's piano concertos for instance. They are partly written out by the publisher because Mozart didn't put it in. He improvised it, so he didn't bother to write it down. And Beethoven got fed up with bad improvisation, so he wrote it all down, but he himself improvised all the time. They trusted themselves in doing that. That has been taken over by popular music now, especially jazz musicians, but in the classical world, it has all but disappeared. Maybe it's starting to come back again, learning to improvise. But you can't use jazz improvisation in my music. That's another language.

ARAM: There are themes in both jazz and classical music, though.

TOMMIE: It's the same thing. But jazz, to me, seems to have been stuck in a very predictable formula that can be so boring to me. I heard a very good jazz performance a few months ago with Monica Dominique and an all-female group who managed to avoid the clichés and make the music really exciting. But sometimes jazz can be so boring. But routine can also be a danger in all sorts of musical genres. Was it Frank Zappa who said, "Jazz isn't dead. It just smells funny"?

ARAM: And wasn't it Anthony Burgess who said, "Jazz is not for listening to but for playing"?

Photo: Lennart Löfberg

Elisabet with Julia and Clara, ca. 1990.

TOMMIE: Sometimes a piece of music is deadly important to you, and then a few years later, it means nothing. And you can't explain why. Bruckner, for example, meant nothing to me until very recently. I used to think he was such a bore, but now Symphony No. 8 sounds like the best thing you could ever think of. The slow part, it sounds like he's waiting for death. And there's a horn part that sounds like it's from a western film.

ARAM: There's music that I like because it has an aroma of the past, a period of your life that is gone now, no other reason. You can enjoy something and also think it's banal or flawed. Beyond that, can you ever come up with a universal field theory for quality?

TOMMIE: No, you can't come up with the ultimate theory. When I was in Århus studying classical guitar, I had a Swedish acquaintance, also a guitarist, who believed music should always be safe, take no risks, play the right notes, and so on. He considered Julian Bream to be an eccentric. So, anyway, Manuel Barrueco[57] came to give a master class in Århus, and I was there. Someone in the class was playing a piece, and Barrueco said, "I can't play like this. I'm too pure." I'm too pure! Why was he playing music, then? This is so far from my approach to life and music. If you have that view, I think it'd be better to sit and make clocks instead.

ARAM: Do you think it's better to have your own ideas rather than rely on what other people say?

TOMMIE: It's very difficult to say. I always try to be open to advice if I'm uncertain. And I'm not afraid of criticism, but once I've made up my mind there's nothing to discuss.

ARAM: Can you teach someone to be creative? Or can you only teach them how to be critical of their work?

TOMMIE: That's an interesting question. Creativity is a method you learn and one that doesn't necessarily involve high intelligence. For me, it's partly a matter of remaining a child and the ability to play, to do unexpected things, to take unexpected turns, however serious you may be. And it's learning to live with high risks. Not everyone is suited for that. At first, when I compose, I say yes to everything, every idea, and let them come and go. Then, there comes this moment when you focus. I have to pull myself together and get it done. You have to be able to play like a child, and that's when the unexpected ideas come in. I'm writing this piece now for the Royal Stockholm Philharmonic Orchestra, and I'm living in one or two years of total insecurity as to how it'll

57 Manuel Barrueco (1952–) is a Cuban classical guitarist.

turn out—whether it'll turn out. I'm so used to living under these conditions, being confused and not knowing how the result will turn out for months. It's part of the creative process, I think.

ARAM: Do you ever draw any inspiration from minimalist composition?

TOMMIE: I must admit that each time I hear a minimalist piece, I feel slightly stupider. When I was a child in the hospital, and they were examining my intestines, in order to cope, I used to repeat melodies to myself to get rid of the pain. In a way, that was a kind of minimalism. It's a sort of hypnotic thing that repeats, and you get into a certain state. I feel more like a maximalist in that sense. Though I have done some minimalistic pieces, like *Meditation*, and there is a repeating structure there.

ARAM: The great majority of music in history, apart from European tradition, was minimalist.

TOMMIE: I just don't feel drawn to it. And I do think it has to do with the printing press and music publication in early modern Europe—that enabled composers and performers to go beyond what could be preserved in the memory and allowed them to be much more complex.

ARAM: That's an interesting observation, but then again, there were Brahmins, even in the twentieth century, who could chant the entirety of the Vedas off by heart. So, it can't be the human memory. How does mass printing affect the complexity of composition?

TOMMIE: Maybe not everyone has that sort of memory. Once it was written down, you could do something much more complex with the choir in the monastery. Machaut is a particular example of a quantum leap in this sense.

ARAM: How would you place yourself in the world of contemporary music?

TOMMIE: I leave that to others. It feels pretentious, and it doesn't fit into my world. The most important thing is that I can write the music I hear within me. Of course, I'm happy if my music is perceived as moving or beautiful, but not in a sort of bourgeois complacency. Beauty has more aspects than butter and sugar. Perhaps I'm looking for something both spiritual and physical.

ARAM: Do you ever listen to music by others as you compose?

TOMMIE: Never when I'm actually composing; then, I need to be completely undisturbed. Mostly, I listen at nighttime to cleanse myself so I can sleep—so I can have something else to dream about. Once in the 1990s, I said to Erik Wallrup, "This music I'm writing is terrible. It has no quality in it." And Erik said, "Have you listened to any of your colleagues recently?" That was his advice. Maybe he was being too critical, but it put me into a good humor. [*Laughs.*] No, I can't really listen to any other music when I'm composing. So much concentration is required when I'm writing, I just can't.

ARAM: Most composers would not describe their compositions as an interior journey, even if their personalities do end up in the work.

TOMMIE: I need to be alone, like a turtle. I need to take time and be silent and all that—to go into myself. Anything that comes to me, I just accept it as it is. And suddenly, I come to a point where I'm involved and don't think. I can't even think. I just let something else take control of me. That's where the interior journey starts, I think. All sense of time and pain dissolve, and I'm into this new world, which takes time to explore. It's very taxing, and sometimes I have to wash my face with ice-cold water. But those moments don't necessarily produce music of high quality. I think it's important to distinguish creativity and research. Sometimes, when you feel you're discovering something, it doesn't come off; you have to set it aside for a while, come back to it, go through it again and again, and finally, there is something you can use. You have to reach the areas that are silent and wake them up.

ARAM: Is there an interior landscape, one that is the same each time you visit?

TOMMIE: Some days, I just can't grasp it. Exterior things can affect me—chores, pain. These are distractions, but once you're in there, it's fantastic. When you reach that point, nothing else exists.

20: DELIUS

ARAM: What does Delius mean to you now?

TOMMIE: He's just—he's an important thing to me, but the music itself is . . .

ARAM: A stepping-stone?

TOMMIE: A stepping-stone, maybe. I don't listen to Delius very often now. I'm very selective about it. When I haven't heard anything of him for a long time and hear something, I think it's the most beautiful music ever written. There are still many things there that speak to me, and I like when he goes beyond himself, like in the *Arabesque* and parts of the *Requiem* and *North Country Sketches,* where he stretches the boundaries of tonality. And there's this opera, *Fennimore and Gerda,* that was very unflattering in many ways, and the ending . . . it was so unexpected. Some of the *Requiem* is dogmatic, where he tries to persuade you to be anti-religious—they're unconvincing, just dull mastery. But at the ending, when he's talking about eternal renewal, then I believe every note. It's worth noting that up until 1915, the critics considered Delius a modernist. He despised the bourgeoisie. When he was at home in Bradford as a child, he had to stand up in a black velvet suit and play the violin for well-to-do members of the upper middle class who were guests in the home. They didn't know the difference between a violin and a tennis racket, he said.

ARAM: *Requiem* and *Arabesque* are some of the least performed of his works.

TOMMIE: Fenby loved the *Requiem* most of all, and he thought the *Arabesque* was also one of the best. And as I mentioned earlier, here he's approaching early Schönberg. Delius had a certain way of constructing melodies. Fenby described it as a prose melody, and it's particularly noticeable if you listen to the solo concertos and the vocal pieces. Those have influenced me a great deal. I'm thinking about *Sea Drift* with Walt Whitman's texts about a young man who reaches maturity when he becomes aware of the demanding conditions of life by watching a couple of seagulls nesting. One day, the she-bird flies away, never coming back. The he-bird calls day and night but in vain. That has left a deep impression in me.

ARAM: I don't think of your compositions as having narratives, per se. Maybe one or two of them.

TOMMIE: Not narrative, but sometimes the melodies are formed as prose melodies, like Delius. In *Intenso Animi,* there are a few things that echo Delius, but really very little. Perhaps more in the serenade. I think your native language—be it Swedish, English, or French—is an ingredient in the structure. Janáček very consciously used Czech intonation in his melodies, you know? Delius had a very personal language that was only his own. He was really off the main track of continental classical music. Debussy was expansive and had a school, while Delius never formed a school. Look at [Philip Arnold] Heseltine. He tried to copy Delius and got stuck in a cul-de-sac. I never thought of copying Delius and never used his chords or anything like that. First of all, Delius rarely expressed anxiety or anger; he was hopeless at that. When he tried, it sounded unconvincing. He was more successful when he was celebrating life and nature or expressing sadness over the perishability of these things. What I did was to identify with the sadness that drove Delius and the way he beautified sadness and longing, and transform that into my own language. Almost everything of Delius' has a slow pace; same with mine. He was a catalyst, Delius. There is something in the slowness that attracted me, same with the early baroque music that I liked and the tragic pieces by Dowland. Do you think I sound like Delius?

ARAM: No. Not at all.

TOMMIE: Do I sound like anyone to you?

ARAM: As I've said here and there, Bruno Maderna. Except that he's actually writing twelve-tone music—but the note-clustering and the use of central tones from which notes gravitate has certain affinities. There's something you and he have in common there. That's just an example.

TOMMIE: I do see what you mean about that Maderna piece you played for me.

ARAM: Delius seems to have been caught between the Romantic era and the Modern era.

TOMMIE: He called twelve-tone "the wrong-note school."

ARAM: Not just musical modernism, and not just in the arts. Technology, industry, everything was changing fast. Old Europe was slipping away before the eyes of the artists and composers. I think you can see something similar in Philippe Smit's paintings,[58] capturing these vignettes of Old Europe before they're gone—and he knows they'll be gone. Smit had this yearning for Old Europe—its colors, these obscure roads through the forest that open into village settings, vagabonds who wandered an illegible landscape, windows that look out onto the moonlit woods, châteaus and castles—things he must have felt would soon be nothing but memories in the modern world. I think many of his canvases were ways of capturing his own memories. I hear something similar in Delius, as he lived through the wars and watched things changing in the modern world. Grez-sur-Loing is a place where life is still slow to change, and maybe Delius liked it for that reason.

TOMMIE: He wasn't popular among the villagers. [*Laughs.*] He rarely spoke to them. But no, you're right. There is an air of sadness in the work, an era that is slipping away, gone. You know, I think the first movement of the *North Country Sketches*, the winter landscape, is almost like a mystical initiation. And yes, there is a very specific atmosphere in that village, Grez, a mixture of dullness and beauty. Fenby also talked about that. He said it was as if the village was surrounded by a force field from which you could not escape. I understand why Scandinavian artists went there—Strindberg, Carl Larsson, Bruno Liljefors, Ernst Josephson. There was a Swedish colony there, maybe still. Larsson did his best paintings there, his breakthrough paintings. Strindberg had the famous quarrel with

58 Philippe Smit (1886–1948) was a Dutch painter of landscapes and portraits collected by Rev. Theodore Pitcairn.

his wife, a turning point in his life. Delius was more sensual and more life-affirming, à la Nietzsche, but with sadness at the same time. It woke something up in me.

ARAM: Where was Delius at his worst?

TOMMIE: It feels presumptuous of me to say, but in those early pieces, he hadn't really found himself. He didn't find himself until he was nearly forty. Before that, there is so much Grieg and Strauss in the music. I'm thinking of *Paris, Song of a Great City* and the piano concerto; *The Magic Fountain* lacks identity. His piano concerto is a failure, and he said so himself. It's not him; when he tries to be dramatic or aggressive, it just isn't his scene. There is one exception, the *Florida Suite*. It's well-orchestrated and very inventive. Some parts of *Appalachia* veer close to film music in a way that comes off as thin. Many say it's a fantastic piece of music, but I . . . I don't know. I never listen to those, never ever. But he had to write himself through those in order to find himself. When he got beyond Strauss and focused on his inner self, that was the real Delius. What do you think of that piece, *Appalachia*?

ARAM: Feels like novelty music to me. But so does a lot of that heavy Americana stuff—Aaron Copland and Leonard Bernstein especially. Delius to me is an inconsistent composer, but there are moments of unbelievable depth of solitude and fantasy.

TOMMIE: Sometimes I wonder who I'd be if I hadn't been acquainted with so many people connected with Delius—Fenby and Soldanella—in particular. Their influence was as great as Delius'. I'm very grateful that I came across him at the moment when I was still receptive. Had it happened at a different time in a different

Photo: Christer Strandberg

Tommie Haglund, ca. 1989

place, it might just have passed along. But at that moment, it had such an impact. Delius will always be with me on some level.

ARAM: Has the Scandinavian landscape played any role in your personal history or compositional style, as the English countryside did for Delius?

TOMMIE: I think being brought up by the sea, in Kalmar, was important, as was the mystery of the Swedish forests. There is a John Bauer[59] quality to my memories of the forests. I would never move

59 John Bauer (1882–1918) was a Swedish fairy tale illustrator who also later painted in a cubist style. He drowned during a storm while crossing Vättern. His wife, Esther Bauer (who also drowned in 1918), was a friend of Soldanella's

away from the sea. The mysteries and atmosphere of Öland have been inspiring. There's an otherworldliness there, almost mystical. But no, the inner landscape doesn't look like Scandinavia, if that's what you mean. You've heard Delius' *Song of the High Hills.* There is much of nature and mysticism there. I think that's where he's really at his best in describing nature.

ARAM: What about his *Mass of Life*?

TOMMIE: It was almost a religious experience. It was like an intoxication, hearing certain chord shifts carrying it along. I remember every note of this two-hour work. It contains enigmatic sections where you can hear echoes of Wagner, but it's personal all the way through. In some passages, he reveals the mystic I think he is. No one else but Delius could have written it. *A Mass of Life* is the culmination of his obsession with Nietzsche. It is, you note, a Mass of life, not a Mass of death. But it will never belong to the canon. To be popular with the masses was never his goal. "Am I getting popular?" he wrote to a friend after a concert where his music was applauded. "Beware." [When] I was twenty, twenty-five, thirty, I had to have a portion of Delius every day. I suspect I had an overdose. I spent many years not listening to anything else. Then I heard this new recording of the Double Concerto by Tasmin Little, a piece I didn't understand before, but then I heard her version. I wrote to her saying I thought it was magnificent, that I'd discovered new things, and she was really delighted. I hear Delius so differently now. He sounds more transparent and less complicated to me now.

---

mother. *Esther,* a Swedish TV film from 1986, featured a scene of Philip Oyler burning his wife's canvases.

ARAM: Before, you were describing Delius' *North Country Sketches* as an initiation.

TOMMIE: Yes, the first movement reminds me a bit of Sibelius. You hear long notes in a low register, and gradually, the music becomes more and more animated before it disappears in the same low register. It sounded ghost-like, especially the first time I heard it on 78 rpm disc with surface noise. It's an autumn and winter landscape. There is a spiritual message in that music, and I'm sure if Delius heard me say that, he'd laugh. Delius had a huge interest in the occult when he lived in Paris, but I think he turned away from it.

ARAM: Delius also had a certain interest in the inner landscape, or at least turning inward with his music as metaphor.

TOMMIE: In Delius' case, it's very obvious in some of his pieces. You can really feel him turning inward. Listen to the *North Country Sketches* especially—it's the four seasons, but to me, it's really man's inner seasons.

ARAM: He constructed it to work on multiple levels? Or do you think he composed more intuitively?

TOMMIE: Intuitively but methodically—something he learned as a student in Leipzig. He told Fenby that he never forced composition; he just let the music flow. And he was criticized for not being formal enough. It's very much based on intuition, the heart's unification with thought, the search for another ecstasy.

ARAM: Are you saying you think Delius, through his composition, tapped into something beyond his composition? Maybe there's some connection to Delius' Paris days, his séances, and so on. I'd like to know who he was with in those days besides Strindberg.

Frederick Delius at his piano, ca. 1916.

TOMMIE: Well, I can tell you a bit. And this is not very well known. We know he was acquainted with Munch and sporadically with Ivan Agueli, Paul Gaugin, and Henri Rousseau. Among the composers were Maurice Ravel, William Molard, and Florent Schmidt. Strindberg played the guitar, Molard and Ravel the piano, and Gaugin the mandolin. It was at this time that Delius became interested in astrology and the occult, sometimes with a wink of the eye. Strindberg was in his *Inferno* period, and one evening at the hotel where he stayed, he put all the chairs and tables in the dining room along the wall and put out kettles and placed them in a circle on the floor. Dressed only in a shirt and underwear, he performed an exotic dance around them. He did this to frighten the evil spirits so they wouldn't poison his food. Delius and Munch played a joke on Strindberg by arranging a spiritist séance with a Ouija board or something. The light was turned out, and the three of them, as well a man named Leclerc, sat around a little table holding each other's hands. After ten minutes, there was a fateful silence. The table started shaking and one of the participants asked what message the spirits had for them. It came via letters—the letter A was one knock, B two knocks, and so on. The first letter was M, and for every letter, the tension increased for Strindberg. And with the last letter, the word became *merde*.[60] Strindberg never forgave them.

The interactions between humor and seriousness are not hazardous. We see it in Cleese, who wants to know the whole human psyche. Fenby was of the opinion that Delius and Bartók were two composers whose personalities stood in direct contrast to their work. Bartók was a very friendly and almost shy man, whereas his music was often hard and uncompromising. With Delius, it was the opposite; he was a ruthless man who composed amiable and tender music.

ARAM: Which was around the First World War. There's a theory that the entire Western world changed forever in the year 1910.

TOMMIE: I'm not sure about that, but after the Second World War no one wanted any more emotional outbursts. They couldn't bear it. They thought they had to create a completely new thing, and they did liberate art in a way, but by the '60s, it had become like a straightjacket. Everything's been done. Once you've gone that far, where are we? People stopped listening. You can afford not to have an audience when the economy is going up, like after the wars.

But then you have Arvo Pärt.

---

60 The French word for excrement.

ARAM: He's sort of a serialist counter-revolutionary. The anti-Schönberg, in certain ways.

TOMMIE: I don't agree with that completely. He's writing serialist music but with Middle Age techniques into an a-religious, materialist world. I think Schönberg will always be a footnote for major audiences, despite the fact that almost every composer after the mid-century was influenced by him. He wrote some masterly tonal works, also. He was an extremely interesting figure and a gifted painter. And he was aware of his place in history and the limits of his horizons. I think at the beginning of the century—or 1910, as you say—he had reached an emotional cul-de-sac and could only branch out by re-inventing the tonal system. But it was in the air. The Norwegian composer Fartein Valen, who was Sven-Eric's teacher, was on the same track around the same time.

ARAM: Delius was no fan of Schönberg's work. His own highly wrought work is more about the chaotic vitality of life and nature. Many of his concertos are like symphonic paintings, fine and innovative . . . and certain others I find really saccharine.

TOMMIE: Yes, he was really fascinated by Schönberg's *Harmonielehre*. But as a whole, I'm not sure. The music of Delius doesn't play itself, and it's not technically easy for orchestras to play, even the sugar-pieces. I think that Delius will continue to be seen as one of the most colorful and inventive composers of the early twentieth century—an international artist who found himself in the midst of the complex rise of modernism. He said firmly that he was not a British composer. And it is impossible for him to be accepted by academia.

21: ANXIETY

Compositions: Beyond Farewell

ARAM: What's the relationship between reality and anxiety? Does life feel more "real" while in anxiety?

TOMMIE: There is an anxiety that overpowers everything. I would say more surreal than real. It twists reality into a state where your whole body reacts. Often, when I'm driving alone in traffic, it whispers back. Or sometimes it's like an echo.

ARAM: Anxiety about anxiety?

TOMMIE: Exactly. It's like scar tissue. It doesn't clarify it. It's overpowering. It even takes over sound.

ARAM: Do you think if you didn't worry about anxiety, listened to it rather than fight it, that it would provide a sense of clarity or another form of awareness?

TOMMIE: No. Anxiety is part of being human, and it has a purpose. It tells you something is threatening you from the inside, and you have to reflect upon things in your life. Now, I live with traces of this time that I have to handle, and I'll never be completely free from anxiety. When it comes, I just pat myself on the shoulder and say, OK, I have anxiety now. It's a pity, but it will pass. You can feel a different kind of anxiety that way because you're so deep inside yourself—you're trying to get as close as you can to some of these feelings to describe them—but that's different from panic attacks.

ARAM: Do you think you can, through art, make things more real? Pain, joy, anxiety? Or do you find art to be limited, and that it always is pale compared to experience?

TOMMIE: Certain composers make something like holograms of emotions; I want to go much deeper than that. In some parts of Bruckner's Symphony No. 9, which was only fully orchestrated recently, there's a real palpable anxiety there. That's opened new doors for me.

ARAM: Going into yourself and experiencing joy or fear or whatever you find—these things can be made real and permanent, not more dangerous, but more graphic in a way, through art, through music?

TOMMIE: Yes. My comedian friend, Thomas Petersson, came here recently and listened to the end of the violin concerto. He doesn't drink coffee because it makes him feel panicky, and when he heard the violin concerto, he said that was exactly how I feel in a panic. [*Laughs.*] Also, there was a neurologist here around the time the violin concerto had just arrived from the record company because his daughter took lessons with Elisabet. We sat listening to it, and he looked at his arm and the hair was standing up. He was, as a neurologist, fascinated by it.

ARAM: Almost as if you sonically translated your own anxiety into a livable experience and, thus, made your inner self legible.

TOMMIE: I often wonder what goes on inside a person at a time like that.

ARAM: Is there any music you've written in which you're trying to escape from the inner self?

TOMMIE: I don't know what that would be good for. Sometimes, people get stuck in an almost neurotic positivism that makes life unreal. And these things I do my best to avoid. The only acceptable condition today is happiness. Emotional ruts are part of life, and people are encouraged to take tablets. Public photographs are always our happiest moments. See what a happy life I have.

ARAM: What happened when you moved beyond the violin concerto?

TOMMIE: Bill Marsh said my violin concerto was terrible; the chords were terrible, anxiety-stricken, dissonant, and so harsh he couldn't take it. But that's my answer to Delius' Violin Concerto. I couldn't do it another way. I actually didn't think of it as an answer to Delius when I was writing it. The piece was to be a summary of my life. So when I chose the Dowland passage, I was thinking of my youth—the most beautiful music I knew from my youth. My final statement is almost like the counting down of the final clock. I remember having "parallel worlds" going on at the end as well, three simultaneous things, actually: Dowland is there, singing desperately to stay alive; and an early baroque technique, a passacaglia; and I wanted to create an otherworldliness. If you just have the Dowland without the chords and the passacaglia—the tune itself—you have a perfect renaissance piece. They did that while they were recording it! It was quite a liberation to hear that.

ARAM: What do you mean by "parallel worlds"?

TOMMIE: When I start composing, I am in another world. Sometimes, it takes me really far in, an endless world hovering within me—like listening to a radio, and I'm trying to tune it in clearly, trying to reach it.

ARAM: I also think there are some certain threads that run between Swedenborg and this aspect of the music.

TOMMIE: Of course. I remember reading the dream book.[61] Portions of it were read on Swedish Radio when *Intensio Animi* premiered. Extracts from the dream book were read by different actors like Göran Bergendahl. And they're actually in the published score as well—the visions Swedenborg experienced and how anxiety-ridden he was. It can be both terrifying and uplifting to think there are spirits around you always who can hear and guide you.

ARAM: Why is that terrifying?

TOMMIE: I don't know, I just felt, who is around me? Am I listening to somebody now? Is someone influencing my thoughts? Am I thinking my own thoughts, or is it someone else who is bending around inside me? And as Soldanella said about the medium, you don't know who is talking *through* her. What Swedenborg did at that time was to help me take control.

ARAM: What do you think the music would be like if you'd never read Swedenborg?

TOMMIE: It's impossible to answer. But I was anxious to create an inner universe that would be unassailable, and it's like

---

61 Lars Bergquist, ed. *Swedenborg's Dream Diary,* translated by Anders Hallengren (Royersford: Swedenborg Foundation, 2024).

that still—like walking into a chamber where everything is fragile and at the same time indestructible. Like a sanctuary for the soul.

ARAM: And musically?

TOMMIE: Perhaps I would have been tempted to go into twelve-tone or Boulez mathematical things with rhythm.

ARAM: It's interesting to hear you say that because it sounded to me as if you were already seeing this style of composition as personally inauthentic by the time you reached Århus, which was well before you discovered Swedenborg. You think you might have headed in that opposite direction anyway?

TOMMIE: I'm not sure I would have had the confidence to ask myself, what is it I want to say? Otherwise, I might have written all these pieces just to learn, or to show how clever I am, or how clever I'm not—never pieces that point to feelings or states of mind. But again, I'm only speculating. I had this almost mysterious commission to write for the Swedenborg 300th Jubilee when nobody knew anything about me. This was a year or two after I came across Swedenborg, and I had stopped playing the guitar. I had read the Martin Lamm biography.[62] I read the *Dream Diary* very, very thoroughly. I could connect Swedenborg's *Dream Diary* with my own anxieties. He was a door-opener in that way—very important.

ARAM: How often do you read Swedenborg these days, and what do you tend to pick up?

TOMMIE: About three books a year, sometimes more. *Conjugial Love, Heaven and Hell,* sometimes, *Tremulations*. I think he was

62 *Emanuel Swedenborg: The Development of His Thought* by Martin Lamm, first published in 1915, republished in English translation by the Swedenborg Foundation in 2000.

really onto something with that one. Some days, I have doubts and think that when I die everything will be just black, like before I was born. Nothing. I was with someone recently who was dying, and it was just like a piece of music fading out. There was a stillness, and that's how I've been ending most of my pieces. Nothing dramatic. But dying doesn't terrify me now as it did before. When I was a child, it did so extremely.

ARAM: *La Rosa Profunda* was part of a song cycle you wrote in 2007, but then you finally orchestrated it in 2016.

TOMMIE: Joachim Gustafsson insisted for a long time that I should orchestrate the last movement in the song cycle. There are very dense chords, but it's a romantic piece, really. I wanted it to be as transparent as possible for the listener. Erik expressed some concern about submitting it to the festival in Stockholm. It's like the old austerity I was attracted to has changed, but I don't want to say it's lost its grip on me. I write what I want to hear. But apart from this, Erik is one of the few I really listen to regarding advice. He has such a subtle understanding of my music.

ARAM: Speaking of Joachim, he has been important to you, both by helping to establish the biennial Haglund Festival and as a conductor.

TOMMIE: In a lifetime, most people come and go. I met Joachim in 1991, and since then, we have collaborated more or less all the time. We share the same romantic passion for life as well as music. I love his seriousness combined with wit and sharp intellect. He is a superb conductor and profoundly solid as a friend. Joachim and Anders Wilhelmsson—also a wonderful friend and musician—instigated the Tommie Haglund Festival in 2016. Musicians

Photo: Kike Barona

Joachim Gustafsson conducting Cesar Franck's Symphony in D minor, Orquesta Filarmónica de Bogotá, Bogotá, Columbia, 2017.

and symphony orchestras come to Halmstad to perform my music and music by composers who have influenced me. Joachim is the artistic director, and Anders is in charge of the music in Halmstad's largest church.

ARAM: We were talking before about rock bands who release this really charged stuff in their teenage years and then make the mistake of reforming at age forty-five when they're working in a bank office and don't feel alienated anymore. And the results are invariably boring. I think the worst thing you can do is not let your art change with you. I know people will misunderstand me when I say this, but I really think you are doing with classical composition what a lot of punk bands were doing in 1977. You're touching on the same things, really, except that maybe you're not trying to be deliberately rude and tear down society. But the sense of despair and alienation are so similar.

TOMMIE: I understand the comparison. That's what I'm continuing to do. There's no way for me to do anything else; I simply can't. If I will survive at all, mentally, as a composer, I have to follow this instinct—and this love; it's a matter of love as well.

ARAM: Maybe all this is just the first phase. What will the next phase sound like? Maybe something much different from what you're doing now. What are the new compositions sounding like?

TOMMIE: They're not causing me the same kind of pain. They're warmer. There's more warmth in the chords. I had hardly allowed that before because I wanted this sharpness, this knife-edge, like hitting you where it hurts the most. I have within me the power of a monster when it comes to music. But my aim is for the music to be richer and have a wider emotional span but the same seriousness.

ARAM: But did you want to create a specific effect for the audience, or directly experience empathy?

TOMMIE: Wake them and shake them up—that's what I wanted to do. To have them stirred, moved, and explore areas within themselves they didn't think they had access to. That's all an afterthought, because when you're writing music, you don't think like that. I don't even care where or if they play my music. My only concern is the composition and that every note has a meaning. People die having only discovered a fraction of what's inside them. To be able to forget time, like as a child. You never know what other people are going to feel. I don't even know what you see when you look out the window.

ARAM: Would you want people's expectations to drive decisions about composition?

TOMMIE: I don't know what the audience's expectations are, but sometimes I want to provoke just for the sake of it, but on my conditions.

ARAM: And what if you do lose your audience? Just continue?

TOMMIE: I'd have to accept it.

ARAM: It would be worse to force the intensity.

TOMMIE: I couldn't. If the intensity diminishes, then I stop writing music.

ARAM: It doesn't appear you'll be slowing down anytime soon. In fact, now there are several things going on at once. You're beginning a piano concerto, a work for guitar, and you've just finished a symphony. And as well, a rather unexpected, at least to me, collaboration with Per Gessle. How did that come about?

TOMMIE: Well, it all started with us meeting coincidentally at a coffee shop here in Halmstad. It was just a couple of months before the last Haglund Festival [2019] in Stockholm. This was in January, and he was on his way to a rehearsal for a summer tour with his pop group. We got talking, and I suggested he come to the festival. He suggested likewise that I come see his group, Gyllene Tider. I went back home and thought, oh well, he was probably just being polite, but then I opened the laptop and there was a message from him. So, he was there for one of the festival days and also, I think, for one of the rehearsals. The music he was hearing was really atonal, and I feared he would find it too much and leave during the intermission. But he didn't, and we had a conversation after the concert, and then we continued talking for a while.

Meanwhile, I was working with Lars Nordin on marketing for the festival. Lars is Per's brother-in-law, and he suggested we all get together. So, the three of us met at Per's hotel for dinner. I told him the story about Majken Ohlsson, and he talked about his life. It went late into the night; I didn't expect it to be so late. But during that evening, we decided to collaborate, meaning Per would provide the lyrics and I the music. We were both scared about it, honestly—that it was going to be a fiasco. He was thinking, what if Haglund writes something too extreme? And I'm thinking, what am I to do with pop lyrics? And sure enough, he sent me a text that was a Roxette song, and I couldn't work with it. So, I wrote back and said it was impossible. So, four hours later, a new text arrived, and it was great! It's about age and disappointment and questioning one's choices in life. Someone I know nearly burst into tears when I showed it to him because it fit his life so well.

This was also the time I was reconciling with Bo Strömberg, and one night I came home and wrote a simple tune that was to reflect on his importance to me. I didn't know what to do with it. It was tonal, and the emotions were close to the surface. At first, I thought I could insert it into the symphony, but then it hit me that it fit perfectly with Per's lyrics, down to the last word, and practically without adjustment. So, there's an orchestral introduction. Seeds of this melody are inserted in the symphony as well. It's a tune of gratitude, I would say. So, I wondered how Per would like it. He turned up here; Anders Wilhelmsson came over to play it for him. His response was quite positive, and I was happy with it, too. That's how it came about. The Royal Philharmonic will do it with Emmy Christensen.

ARAM: What would you say the piece consists of?

TOMMIE: The introduction is derived from material I initially laid down for the piano concerto but then decided not to use—impressionistic harmonies, Delian. That's the first two or three minutes. The tune itself is both sad and happy. And then there's a conclusion. So, it's a combination of my usual chords with a tonal structure. Now that I'm thinking about how to write the piano concerto, I was thinking at first that it might be fully tonal.

ARAM: Is the piano concerto a commission?

TOMMIE: Yes, from the Gothenburg Symphony Orchestra, for Niklas Sivelöv, the pianist. When I started, as I said, I thought I was going in a tonal direction, but I had to start all over again many, many times before I found what I was looking for. It's a very mystical, atmospheric, and enigmatic dimension I'm going into right now with my music. I had a chorale in mind—something elevated and dramatic. It's ended up with an exploration of clusters—to find tonality in clusters—very dense sounds with a melody in them. This creates, for me, an unexpected softness and tension, but after a week, I might be onto something else. Earlier, the mysticism was entwined with anxiety, but there's something more enigmatic at work now that is taking it further.

ARAM: What do you mean?

TOMMIE: A dense impressionism, beyond Scriabin. Anyway, as I said, I had a lighter touch in mind, but it was impossible. The concerto is dedicated to Lars Nordin. He creates a peaceful calm around himself while at the same time engaging in a burning creativity. Also, he brought Per and me together.

ARAM: How can I approach the piano concerto within classical music? Where will it be found historically?

TOMMIE: All the music you hear you can relate to something else. I don't think about other composers much anymore. I'm thinking only about inner development. This time, the piece won't be anything like it was when I began it.

ARAM: What can listeners anticipate from the new piece for guitar, *Beyond Farewell*? This is a reimagining of a piece you wrote in 2004.

TOMMIE: Yes, it's the same piece but with some alterations, a new chorale-like section, and a new ending. So, it's an expansion. Everything in the piece was volatile, and John Mills wished there would be a redemption. I didn't at all agree, but John insisted, so I thought I would give it a chance. It took a long time before it felt right. My father died in the middle of the process, and through this, a reconciliation—and forgiveness—occurs at the end of the piece. Julian Bream also died during the process, so I dedicated it to him, as well as John and Bo. John and I sat for hours playing variations on what I composed. Now, I'm waiting for John to record the piece on Julian Bream's guitar.

22: INFINITY IN THE MOMENT

Compositions: Symphony

ARAM: We were talking before about the cello concerto being a final statement or *allkonstverk*, for you. Now you've written a new symphony and life has gone on; you didn't die, and there are always new things to express, but do you think the symphony goes as deep as the cello concerto, or will it achieve something else?

TOMMIE: When I started the symphony, I thought it would be much brighter, less demanding, more peaceful. And in some ways, it is, but also not—because there's a new kind of tension. Maybe I've expanded my abilities to walk between rooms inside myself and open new doors that I've seen but not known how to open. Parts are almost tonal, and parts are made of free tonality. Parts are just solo instrument, parts are instrument dialogue, and other parts are hugely orchestral. It could have been called a concerto for orchestra.

ARAM: There are parts of the symphony, especially the way it changes from section to section, that I can't say I understand yet. The shifting of atmospheres.

TOMMIE: You don't have to understand everything. There are parts of this symphony I've written that I don't even understand myself, and I wondered if I could allow myself to publish music I myself don't understand logically. But I think that's the point. These things have to be there. It's incredibly taxing, as it often is in life. Sometimes, it's been devastating—other times, very enjoyable, and the music flows with a certain amount of relief. I'd like to think of this symphony as more all-embracing than the cello concerto, but I can't know that. After the premier, I decided to rework certain parts and invite more incandescence and impressionism and really pinpoint these moments—a sense of consolation combined with sensualism and warmth. I want to think that the symphony will be more accessible than the cello concerto, but who am I to demand that? Claes-Goran's death in the middle of it certainly affected the outcome.

ARAM: When you say "devastating," do you mean there were moments when you felt the work would never come together artistically, or painful memories that were dredged up, or something else?

TOMMIE: I felt the music moving in a threatening direction toward something odious. Some invisible threat, a terrible anxiety hanging in the air—nothing I could visualize, but it materialized as sound: chords I'd never heard before in my life, very difficult to render. But there are also some peaceful passages, like sacred music, and also some lush romanticism. In the intense parts, it felt like my body was disappearing in anxiety and panic. And in the reworked version, I wanted more of this—I wanted masses of sound like pillars of light. I felt a noise like a threatening clock ticking on the wall the whole time. I didn't want the symphony to be like that when

I started writing. I thought it would be much more peaceful, like *Serenata per Diotima,* but I couldn't control it. It had its own life. I had to fight against the material. It was sometimes difficult to take control of the process. But in the end, it feels balanced.

ARAM: Are there parts of the symphony that reflect moments of real-time, such as Claes-Goran's death? Put another way, is the symphony an artifact of its own composition?

TOMMIE: Difficult to answer. When I started working on the symphony, Jöran Persson, a fine choir leader here in Halmstad, offered his time to transcribe the symphony in the Sibelius music program. I have zero knowledge about how to do this, and Jöran's patience was seemingly limitless. I called him late at night and asked for changes. When a new friend supports you, the process becomes more than just music. If Jöran saw himself through my eyes, he'd know how much I appreciate him.

Almost the minute I finished the symphony, my father died. I had the message he was dying, of course, but I was on my way home from finishing transcribing the score with Jöran when my mother phoned me and said, "Your father will die at any moment." I came to think of our final phone calls—he was so proud that I'd managed with so little of his support. We never really understood each other, he and I. We talked about my music on some occasions. He said he was sincerely moved, as you'd want your parent to be. He could be enormously kindhearted, but also he will remain an enigma to me. It's heartbreaking and almost uncanny his life should end on the same day I put down the last note on my symphony. Thus, it marks an ending to a part of this whole story.

I thought of Claes-Goran many times while writing the symphony and Eric Fenby, of course. It's no coincidence that the opening of the symphony is a lonely flute, and then the motif repeats off-stage with a lonely trumpet at the end of the symphony—that was him, the trumpet was his instrument. I told the trumpet player for the recording to pretend he was standing alone in a field at night, playing to the stars.

ARAM: The symphony has a narrative structure, but also there are pauses in the score where soloists are free to improvise.

TOMMIE: The Danish conductor and composer, Bo Holten, said when he read the score that there is a *cantus firmus* running through the entire piece. There are sections where it's like reaching a state of exhaustion, where you have to either pause for a minute or let everything go to let things happen as they will. I give them clues, and they have notes to play, but they have to be responsible for a little while. The sections are no more than forty seconds. The improvisations are just there to prolong the moment.

ARAM: Why is there no other title besides "Symphony"?

TOMMIE: I couldn't come up with any words to put on it. I don't mean it's abstract music. It just means I couldn't get there. Like when Delius said to Philip Oyler that he'd be disappointed if he saw the flowers in the sunset because, in his inner world, it was so much more beautiful. There were so many things flooding my mind and too many things impossible to describe.

ARAM: It's a fifty-minute piece. This will be a demanding experience both for the performers and listeners.

TOMMIE: The commission was for a twenty-five to thirty-minute piece, but when I started to write and visualize things, it got longer, and I said to hell with the contract. I didn't think I could write a piece in a single movement, holding the intensity from the first moment to the last, like Bruckner. You need to think in long time spans, and I was doubting myself, doubting whether I could create a complex, sustained symphony. I'm just glad it didn't collapse. At times it felt like it would. Recently, I looked at Beethoven's *Hammerklavier Sonata,* which is a piece that is always bordering on collapse. The fugues are enormously brutal, and the way he's handling the sonata form is sometimes bizarre, but he manages because of his intellectual capacity to hold it together. One small mistake and the whole thing would have collapsed. The last movement is almost impossible—so many counter-subjects and so many shifting atmospheres. My symphony aside, I have a reverence for Beethoven, particularly in these moments where he's transcending logic but still manages to come back in one piece. It's like he's gone far out in the universe and come back unharmed. With my limited abilities, all I could do was not let my symphony collapse.

ARAM: [*Laughs.*] This is the first major work you've written since you were healthy again. Are there new structures and sounds here, or perhaps more mature variations on the ones you've focused on since the beginning?

TOMMIE: The same old subjects are still there: eternity, annihilation, illusions, helplessness, and destiny. And also gratitude.

ARAM: Destiny. Tell me more about that.

TOMMIE: For six years, because of a stupid misunderstanding, I hadn't seen Bo Strömberg. I couldn't understand why—disappointment mixed with anger many times. One day, when my grandchild and I sat at the coffee shop, Bo stepped in. "Shall we leave?"

I asked Charlie. "No, I want to sit here with my jigsaw puzzle," she said. I turned ice-cold. After a while, Bo stepped up with a big smile, and I asked him to sit down. It took thirty seconds to clear up the misunderstanding. And I realized we'd be friends as long as we both exist. I went home thinking about this and how easily things can go wrong, and how painful it is when an important person in your life suddenly disappears. Suddenly, a passage of melancholy built up to a crescendo. What am I to do with this music? Then, it became clear it was to be incorporated into the symphony. That an experience can be reformulated into music was nothing new to me, but I got an opportunity to express the immense power of atonement. We cannot exist without facing challenges and facing each other.

ARAM: Destiny. I used to think it was a concept that only applied to the arts.

TOMMIE: There is so much around us that is unknown—like there is a protective shield. Looking back on one's life, it's easy to wonder, "How much was already decided, and how much depends on the choices I've made?" I would never have managed without Elisabet as an unfailing support. It's impossible to try and formulate how much she has meant to my music.

Another thing is humor. Being able to pendulate between humor and deepest seriousness has made me better equipped to handle everything in life. One thing can't exist without the other. Beauty without pain can't exist either. I have sometimes wondered why my music changed so radically around 1988. Soldanella told me after the premiere of *Intensio Animi*, "This is a turning point in your life." I didn't quite get it, myself, then. But she knew. Swedenborg came into my life at the right moment. That gave me new spiritual

Photo: Hans Helander

Tommie Haglund, ca. 1990–1

tools, and at the same time, I found my own musical language. I had several conversations with my friend Goran Appelgren, who was the pastor of the Swedenborgian Church, about whether there can be life after death. This is something you hardly dare to speak about in the Western world today without being ridiculed. Therefore, I wonder if we human beings are intelligent enough to even think about this. Researchers describe how particles can affect one another at enormous distances and that time can go backward, and we are expected to believe it because science tells us so. Niels Bohr said that he who approaches quantum physics for the first time without being shocked hasn't understood it. I compare Swedenborg a bit with Galileo when he asked church men to look into his telescope to see the craters on the moon, and the answer was: we do not need to see because we already know they do not exist.

What we must realize is that we know so little and that we all have innumerable emotions and subtly elusive sensations within us that cannot be verbalized. My life has consisted of trying to transfer my inner self to sonorous music. It has been vitally necessary for me. Maybe everyone can develop thought patterns that make it easier to get in touch with worlds that otherwise would remain unknown. Sometimes, I wonder if life is a dream, and when it's over, we go into another dream. I don't know—that is the only thing with certainty I do know.

Epilogue

POSTLUDE

LISTENERS OF TOMMIE Haglund, his future students, and scholars may wonder from whence came this intense and expressive body of work. What circumstances of his life, what demands, inner and outer, led to *Flaminis Aura* (cello concerto), *Hymnen an die Nacht* (violin concerto), and the *Symphony*? In the music, one feels a great deal of pain, but there is also joy and hope, solemnity and transformation writ large and with baroque passion. Are these passages autobiographical? Psychogeographical? Are they religious affirmations? In this book, the overarching question I put to Haglund is how his compositional style relates to the circumstances of his life, the formative and shaping events, the demands on his physical body, and the timeless inner world that seems to possess him even as he stares across the room at me. Tommie Haglund is that rare composer who can say, "This music is me. I am this music."

Context

There is a perennial argument among theorists as to whether a work of art can be interpreted without an understanding of the life history and cultural climate in which it was created. On the one hand, it is possible, of course, to appreciate a work like Haglund's *Il Regno degli Spiriti* (2001) just as it is possible to appreciate Beethoven's String Quartet No. 14 (1826) without knowing both composers were fighting for their lives as they wrote. It is possible to listen to *Intensio Animi* without knowing about Haglund's appreciation of English composer Frederick Delius, which led to a meeting with Eric Fenby, Delius's amanuensis during the last six years of his life, and who helped the blind and paralyzed composer complete his final works. This, in turn, led to Haglund's friendship with Soldanella Oyler, through whom, in turn, he discovered Emanuel Swedenborg, for whose 300th Jubilee *Intensio Animi* was composed. While these things are, I submit, important, they aren't what drives him to compose. To understand the music, I think we have to look into the viscera, that is, to trace Haglund's midlife descent into a full decade of acute nerve pain and chronic anxiety, or draw back to the vision of eternity he beheld while standing in a dormitory hallway in Århus, or to a chance encounter with Cree and Ojibwe Indians in Canada. The big question is: what ties these things together?

Another question, closer to the surface, is how to place Tommie Haglund in the stream of modern classical music. He is a tonal composer, most of the time, but nothing at all like modern tonal composers such as Rautavaara or Alan Hovhannes. There is an unusual and intuitive fusion of classical and modern atmospherics in Haglund's style, but, like Beethoven, who, in his late quartets, expanded back into the baroque and forward into proto-modern territories at the same time, contemporary influence is nearly absent. Even if lanterns held by Berg and Scelsi do light the night road, Haglund's music is rooted in Western classical tradition, from the Renaissance through Mozart's re-fashioning of baroque dialects and into total chromaticism. Although Haglund instills no notion of spiritual exercise or mantra in his compositions, his use of note-clusters is nonetheless part of a classical style that has attained new rules, with a vocabulary of incompleteness, immediacy, and modernist introspection.

Sweden

It should not be forgotten that Haglund is Swedish and that Sweden, beginning in the 1960s, is the setting for his life and work. Haglund composed his first chamber piece at age eleven, played very briefly in a rock band, and studied classical guitar before going on to devote his life to composition. These early phases are important, each for their own reasons. The rock idiom proved too limited for his expressive demands, but something of its energy and drive has carried over into his compositions. It is also important because he charted a course opposite to that taken by so many young musicians in his generation. The 1970s in Scandinavia saw an explosion of progressive rock and psychedelia, mostly taken in at festivals and on LP records. Much of this movement was pioneered by musicians using their conservatory training expressly to kick themselves free of the nineteenth century. But Haglund went in the opposite direction. Like Delius, who refused to engage with the progressive and, for him, limited styles presented to him in the pre-First World War years, Haglund reached back into classicism and the most expressive of early modern composers for the basis of a language.

The Monday Group (The Måndagsgruppen)

Following the Second World War, music and social life in Sweden underwent profound changes. Pupils of modernist composer Hilding Rosenberg gathered beginning in 1945 to forge a new Swedish music, one free of the antiquated romanticisms and national vernaculars that had dominated the classical scene for centuries. The group met on Mondays at the home of Karl-Birger Blomdahl and thus became known as Måndagsgruppen, the Monday Group. The efforts of the Monday Group would ultimately force into retirement the national romantic establishment and, with it, the orchestra standards of Hugo Alfvén, Kurt Atterberg, Wilhelm Stenhammar, Lars-Erik Larsson, and others in favor of Swedish modernism.

The group's membership shifted over the six years it was active, but among its core members were Karl-Birger Blomdahl, Sven-Erik Bäck, Ingvar Lidholm, Göte Carlid, Eric Ericson, Ingmar Bengtsson, and Sven-Eric Johanson, who, as we have seen, would later serve as a mentor to Haglund. The Monday Group served its members as a forum for study and debate over the works of continental composers such as Schönberg, Hindemith, Krenek, and Berg. Recordings and scores of these composers were not so easy to come by as they are now, so they were shared by members who brought them back from visits to the continent. The Måndagsgruppen was also a special interest group, conceiving, drafting, and finding ways to implement music policy in a country that was increasingly elaborating its social democratic structure. Perhaps we can say they are remembered more for their intellectual and social programs than their musical output. Blomdahl, who was a professor of Composition at the Royal College of Music in Stockholm, as well as Head of Music Programming at the Swedish Broadcasting Corporation, helped generate support for the formative Electronic Music Studio of Stockholm.

Among the Måndagsgruppen's debates was the utility of tonality. Blomdahl was hardly the only composer to wrestle with this in his own compositions. Like most of the members of the group, his works were variously tonal and atonal. Though many composers were turning to electronic means of composition and music production, there was also an increasing interest in what might be called the polar opposite—choral music. Both Blomdahl and Lidholm composed pieces that contained elements of stage drama, religious masses, and contemporary avant-garde work from the continent, such as that of Luigi Nono.[63]

The importance of these six years on the history of Swedish contemporary music cannot be overestimated. It served as a vector for the explosion of new classical and popular musical projects in the next six decades and set the stage for composers like Tommie Haglund to look for inspiration outside of the Swedish modernist scene.

---

63 Luigi Nono (1924–1990) was an Italian twentieth-century composer known for explicitly leftist political content but also complex instrumentation, use of live electronics, and explorations of the concepts of time and the inner world of imagination.

Reverberations

In every composer's work, we can hear reverberations of the artists and thinkers that constitute their lineage—in Haglund's case, Delius, Dowland, and Swedenborg, but it is also possible to feel resonances shared with artists more far-flung that help us, in a way, visualize what we are hearing. Seeing Haglund's music through the lenses of poetry and painting—the inner journeys of Novalis, Munch, Gorky,[64] and Kokoschka[65]—we come closer to understanding the musical searches for vastation—the suffering, despair, abjection, and a thirst for mortal relief. From Haglund's devotions to both the post-Lutheran spiritualism of Swedenborg and the godless materialism of Delius, a tension arises. The influence of Delius, who, like Haglund, suffered from physical pain, is almost inaudible in the composition and its tonality, yet he is there, towering over the composer's personal history and the existential tension that drives much of the work. Dowland is also there, the haunted, elegiac turmoil rising fiery and intense in its clash with the Nietzschean spirit of Delius.

Delius

The importance of Delius to Haglund is immense but difficult to parse, even for the composer himself, who acknowledges the influence goes beyond composition. Delius, as a composer, was

64 Arshile Gorky (1904-1948), born Vostanik Manoug Adoian, was an Armenian-American painter in a highly personal mode of pre-abstract expressionism.

65 Oskar Kokoschka (1886-1980) was an Austrian expressionist painter and poet who, along with his contemporary, Max Beckmann, developed ways of seeing inward and invisible realms.

a paradox. He was both forward-thinking and anachronistic in a world lurching toward Modernity in the lead-up to the First World War. Delius believed European classical music was exhausted, its practitioners endlessly recycling, deriving, and imitating. Though he had long loved Beethoven and Bach, he came to resent them upon the critics' miniaturizing of his own work in their shadows. He also rejected "New Music" and what he called "the wrong-note school" (i.e., twelve-tone, Serialism). Delius believed in creating atmospheres through rich harmonies, yet he often used chords too restless and complex to render immediate appeal. Some of his works even sink to the level of novelty because they are snarling reactions to criticism that his work was not flamboyant enough. He believed emotion was the only way to reach listeners and musical form he defined as the heart's unification with the mind. And yet, as a man and a composer, he was entirely uncompromising.

These contradictions have come to define Delius as a *sui generis* composer—one who, according to *Times* critic Henry Cope Colles, "belongs to no school, follows no tradition, and is like no other composer in the form, content, or style of his music,"[66]—and they had direct effects on Haglund's outlook. Like Delius, the presence of classical influences is not immediately felt in his music. Also like Delius, he is a composer whose work employs a great deal of emotional directness, and through which his audiences can—and in some cases, have no choice but to—empathize with him.

---

66 Henry Cope Colles [writing anonymously], "The Delius Festival: A Retrospect," *The Times*, November 2, 1929.

Arshille Gorky. *The Limit* (1947).

The Limit

Haglund is clear that all his works should be taken with the same degree of seriousness. There should not be lesser works. Even though his work is remarkably varied, there is never an impression that more than one man composed it. There are chronological phases, and there are phases within phases, shifts in color within compositions, but rarely shifts in compositional voice.

His earliest works, less well known to the public at large, betray a sense of wonder at the mystery of existence and eternity and of the inner and outer cosmos but are perhaps otherwise only bound together by their cautious elegance and sincerity. There is a period in the work defined almost entirely by suffering. And there is work that points to the way out of this.

While so much of modern classical music is, in effect, authorless, with no personal experience to be felt through it, Haglund's voice is immediately recognizable. When you face death, not as a distant abstraction, but when your entire body chimes with the fear of dissolution, everything you call for in your art changes. Like Schubert after 1822—the year he learned he was syphilitic—lesser projects gave way to feverish brilliance. Everything looks shallow and feels phony compared to the art you think will redeem and outlive you. Delius, who also spent the last decade and a half of his life suffering from syphilis, first from paralysis and then blindness, nevertheless completed *Songs of Farewell* (1930) with the help of Eric Fenby. *Songs* is a work of twilight reflection and resignation, girded under by levity, nostalgia, and pain. And anxiety, as Jacques Lacan reminds us, never lies.

As with Gorky's *The Limit* (1947), painted during the artist's hastening mortal collapse, Haglund's mature compositions feel driven not only by urgency, but also to a clearer sense of reality, something more real than merely naming and seeing the pain. Gorky: "I have been so lonely, exasperated, and how to paint such empty space—so empty it's the limit!"[67] Haglund's composition *L'Infinito* (1991) was written at a time in his life when anxiety drove all decisions. This piece for solo violin is a catharsis, demanding something absolute from God or Nature. The piece has an

---

67 Julien Levy, *Arshile Gorky* (New York: Harry N. Abrams, 1966), 35.

almost botanical quality, almost blooming into tonality, but instead growing, fighting, and dying.

The Turn Inward

One of the hallmarks of modernism in art is the turn inward and the expression of personal existential concerns. The turn inward, away from empirical observation and toward subjectivity as a foundation for truth, is what connects pre-war poets and painters (Trakl, Rilke, Kandinsky, Kokoschka, later Gorky, and so on) with thinkers such as Jung, Freud, and the much earlier Swedenborg. Although Haglund's compositional method is more traditional, his subjective approach to the very real circumstances of his life recalls the Expressionist era of painting and poetry in that a transcendent unity is sought, or assembled, from the fractured inner world. Unlike the Expressionists, Haglund does not operate as if there is an inherent tension between art and experience. In fact, he, like Swedenborg (who perhaps represents the furthest form of subjective valuation from Expressionism), sees his work as a shadow of a more real inner landscape.

Schönberg and Kandinsky, who lived and worked in this period, both spoke of "spirituality" as the true content of art. This spirituality is very difficult to characterize because it is the very principle of creativity—something entirely apart from science, materialism, and realism, something volatile and self-transforming. Art is the only language—or perhaps metalanguage—capable of answering to it. Even before the Expressionist era, the turn inward had already begun in the hands of Munch, Van Gogh, and Rouault. This is

Oskar Kokoschka. *Portrait of Adolf Loos* (1909).

hardly to say these were the first examples of self-examining art, but rather the first that attempted to penetrate beneath the surface of the visible self into the anxieties of *The Scream* and the alienation of *Adolf Loos,* in the latter of which we see something of the artist expressed through a portrait of someone else.

The Virtuoso

While similar anxieties and illnesses—or sicknesses—may have driven many composers, they were mostly unknown in the actual content of eighteenth and nineteenth-century classical music. These were the centuries of the virtuoso, when individual skill and technique, especially in the *solo concerto*, came to enshrine a cult status for individual performers. Mozart himself was celebrated for his virtuosity as a child performer in a way that would have been totally unknown to baroque musicians. His father described him in the London's *Public Advertiser* of May 21, 1764, as "The greatest Prodigy that Europe or that human nature has to boast of."[68] Although clarity and order were the concerns of the day, at least among the aristocratic patrons of high art, it was not unpopular at this time to view technique as a means to an end, and the performer's task as the full and correct realization of the composer's *Affecte*.[69] Folk and popular genres have always allowed individual performers, or virtuosos, to realize emotions without extensive conservatory training, but perhaps the rise of a fine art with no need for the conservatory (e.g., abstract expressionism, Art Brut, American folk and blues music) is another hallmark of modernism, or at least Modernity. In this sense, at least, Haglund is a modern composer.

Swedenborg

In the string quartet *Il Regno degli Spiriti* (2001), the seemingly simple dialogue of violins, viola, and cello arrives at a sustaining theme—that of the soul's construction of its own timeless habitation. The title is a reference to Swedenborg's *Mundum Spirituum*,

68 Otto Erich Deutsch, *Mozart: A Documentary Biography* (London: Adam & Charles Black, 1965), 34.

69 No adequate term in English conveys the meaning of *Affecte*, as used by eighteenth-century German musicians and critics. Keeping in mind the eighteenth-century context, they should be thought of, rather, as the essential emotions (e.g., joy, grief, anger) that move the soul to compose.

or World of Spirits, the realm entered into immediately upon body-death and where spirits sort out their affections en route to either heaven or hell. The string quartet was written in memory of Soldanella Oyler, Haglund's confidante, who died around that time. It was through Oyler that Haglund began reading Swedenborg, and it was at this time his music direction changed. He underwent a sudden awakening to what would become his own musical language. This perspective positions the string quartet both against and within a post-Enlightenment and pre-psychoanalytic literary tradition—art as a window to the inner life. The subjectivism of European romantics such as Shelley and Novalis, and more generally, Delius and Schumann, reflects a new spiritual course inward and to the East. To understand Haglund, it is important to reflect upon the experiences of Swedenborg and similarly of Jung, whose *Red Book* is filled with visual confrontations with his own unconscious, or what he referred to as the "mythopoetic imagination."

For Swedenborg, the mythopoetic imagination was instead a very real, living world populated by spirits dwelling all around us. There, one's affections build the environment for eternity. In most of Haglund's major works, i.e., the string quartet, the violin concerto, and the cello concerto, the triangular tension between the fragile failing body, the implacable cruelty of Nature, and the possibility of redemption are brought to life. They are rendered from the composer's emotional life into a scheme of tone and color, one not inalienable from Kandinsky's but more understandable in the language of critic Malcolm Cowley, who wrote, "Particle after particle of the living self is transferred into the creation, until at last it is an external world that corresponds to the inner world and has the power of outlasting the author's life."[70]

Suffering and Transcendence

Haglund's string trio, *Sollievo (dopo la tempesta)* (2014), is, like the violin concerto, a work with an episodic but non-repetitive structure. Reaching out of the strings is a voice speaking with the memory of a bitter past. Time flows forward and backward, not mechanically, but as it does in the memory, a simultaneous whole. Strength and hope are, as ever, tempered by moments of stumbling fear and loss, false hopes and shadows. These works are like poems—not narrative poems and not tone poems either—but like Rilke's poems, part plainsong and part synthesis, both hard-wrought and spontaneously generated. The string trio is a work in which we can feel, as in several of Haglund's compositions, a sense of emergence: the poignant relief of triumph over suffering—not conquest, but survival—with the rising of each episode. And with its sinking, still a fearlessness in the face of oblivion, a second triumph over our complex relationship with suffering. *Serenata per Diotima* (2014), Haglund's lullaby to his granddaughter, expresses more fully the emergence from suffering in its recapturing of innocence. But through awakening comes a new and subtle tension, one not dissimilar to the landscape of the string quartet and cello concerto, *Flaminis Aura* (2001), which resumes the question of the mystical apprehension of the spirit, thus signaling an interest in mystical

---

70 Malcolm Cowley, "Introduction," in *Writers at Work: The Paris Review Interviews*, vol. 1, ed. Malcolm Cowley (New York: Viking, 1958), 20.

conceptions of reality. The Latin phrase *flaminis aura* can mean several things, among them something "felt in the air prior to a vision." Is there a world beyond our five senses, through which occasionally traces of information permeate? Or is the world of the spirit ours alone, within us, constructed from a palate of symbols and impervious to the selective forces of Nature?

Daughter of the Voice (2010) builds slowly into a narrative of both complex and simple-sounding chords and instrumental and vocal dialoguing. While on the surface, the subject might seem to be the uncontrollable pain of Mary's empathy for her son on the cross and the subsequent joy of the transfiguration, there is a deeper layer of meaning. As in most of Haglund's major works, beneath the score is a great deal of pain, but this time, it is expressed not so directly as it is in *L'Infinito* and *Intensio Animi*, but allegorically, his voice ranging through in the dialogue of dual soprano vocals—both Mary, one heavenly, one earthly. In the conclusion, they are in unison, reaching a semblance of transfiguration in the melody.

Torment

Ingmar Bergman

> What Johan Borg wanted to say was that he is faced with a "must," an unending torment, toothache. He can't escape it. There's no question, that is, of a gift from on high. No other-worldly relationship. It's just there. A disease. A perversion. A five-legged calf. He takes a very brutal view of his situation.
>
> —Ingmar Bergman discussing the protagonist of his film *Hour of the Wolf*.

What Bergman is addressing in his explanation of his character Johan Borg's torment (played by Max von Sydow) is whether it is also a gift. In the film, Borg is a painter who gives his nightmares a life on paper. He, like all artists, never actually exorcises his demons by making them whole and colorful, but Borg carries on sketching anyway, day after day. Instead of escaping his demons, he enters deeper into their world, with imagination and reality losing distinction. He describes in detail to Alma, his wife, his hours alone as a child locked in a dark closet, where, according to his taunting parents, there lived a small creature that would bite off his toes. Bergman admitted this experience was his own childhood hell, and perhaps he is articulating it in film for the same reason Borg renders his demons on paper. But the question, again, is not whether or how demons are exorcized—or whether by detailing them, they are given an even greater internal life and power—but whether, for their torment, they hold a gift in their hands.

It is difficult to say Borg's demons aren't real without also saying that they are. To claim they aren't real is to personalize them, to relativize them, and ultimately to do no less than disable the Manichaean notions at the root of Judeo-Christian cosmology. But this also locks Borg into his own universe, with no god to cry out to, which means the demons are more than real—they are himself. His nightmares are not illusions but real inner landscapes. And the imagination is not a link to a greater reality; it is the only reality. Borg's art, then, takes on an inner dimension, reconnoitering his imagination, as Jung did, then drawing them in detail in his *Red Book*. It almost seems as if Borg's sketching brings the demons to life in *Hour of the Wolf*, making them more real and detailed when they finally appear at Baron von Merkens' castle.

> The only thing that burns in hell is the part of you that won't let go of your life: your memories, your attachments. They burn them all away, but they're not punishing you, they're freeing your soul. If you're frightened of dying and you're holding on, you'll see devils tearing your life away. If you've made your peace, then the devils are really angels freeing you from the earth.
>
> —Bruce Joel Rubin, from the screenplay of *Jacob's Ladder*; paraphrasing Meister Eckhart's Speech *5b, DW I.*

Munch

Edvard Munch struggled to achieve a technique for rendering the pain he felt and witnessed on a two-dimensional surface without flattening its effect. In an early private journal entry, he wrote, "How should one paint true weeping after nature?—as it was when someone was dissolving in tears innermost—like the weeping of the woman I saw in the hospital for venereal diseases—with the sickly naked baby in her arms. She who had now come to learn that her child was doomed to die from birth."[71] Munch answered his own question in 1902, when finally, after increasingly desperate messages, he submitted to visit the manipulative Tulla Larsen on her boat, where she was reportedly dying of lovesickness for

71 Edvard Munch, *The Private Journals of Edvard Munch: We Are Flames Which Pour Out of the Earth*, ed. and trans. J. Gill Holland (Madison: University of Wisconsin Press, 2004), 89.

Edvard Munch. *Self-Portrait in Hell* (1903).

him—and from the morphine she was injecting to blunt it. What exactly happened, we'll never learn—whose revolver it was, who reached for it first, and who pulled the trigger, but Munch found himself in a room full of smoke and blood—frightening amounts of blood gushing from his right hand; and later in the hospital, where he refused anesthetic. Munch watched carefully as his hand was x-rayed. The doctors sliced into the flesh of his hand to remove the hard splinters of shattered bone. The operation lasted for hours, so Munch said. He felt himself trimmed, pierced, and sewn up. His hand, unbandaged, was a monstrosity. He knocked it against furniture and on the tram. He drank bottles of wine to take himself

Edvard Munch. *Portrait on the Operating Table* (1902–03).

away from the disgusting, useless thing. He isolated himself from those he believed were staring at it, only to stare at it by candlelight at night. The hand became an object of obsession. The two self-portraits that followed the recovery of Munch's use of his fingers (*Self Portrait in Hell*, 1903; and *Self Portrait on the Operating Table*, 1902-03) hide nothing of the pain and self-contempt, opening their subcutaneous expressions like an x-ray; but curiously, in both of these, the hand itself it cropped out.

Delius

Frederick Delius, who corresponded with Munch for three decades, also suffered, in his case, from the deleterious effects of syphilis. The question of whether and how Delius depicted his condition in his music is debatable. Fenby had a theory that Delius found his musical language only when the syphilis began spreading in his body. On the other hand, between 1911 (the year he felt largely recovered from the initial bout of syphilis) and 1917 (the year of his relapse), he was prolific. But after 1924, by which time paralysis and blindness had set in, and until the arrival of Eric Fenby in 1928, he produced next to nothing. But after that, as the syphilis took hold of him, he composed the best work of his life. Delius' primary biographers tend to avoid speculating about this, and Delius himself spoke only reservedly about his condition or its effect on the music. Toward the end of his life, when most visitors were turned away from the house at Grez-sur-Loing, Philip Oyler was among the few permitted to sit with Delius. One evening, they were in the garden as "the declining rays of the sun were falling upon a border in such a way that the flowers seemed to have become more ethereal than real."[72] Oyler remarked on this, saying he wished Delius could see what he saw and immediately felt ashamed for making such a tactless remark to a blind man. But Delius replied "that he had no regret that he could no longer see them, for he might be disappointed if he could. They might, he said, be less beautiful than they were in the sight of his imagination."[73]

There is no such thing as a problem without a gift for you in its hands. You seek problems because you need their gifts.

—*Richard Bach,* Illusions

---

72 Philip T. Oyler, "Delius at Grèz," *The Musical Times* 113, no. 1551 (1972): 447.

73 Oyler, "Delius at Grèz," 447.

Underground

In the waning days of the eighteenth century, Novalis[74] opened the door to a new and unexplored world in literature and the arts. His lyrical cycle *Hymnen an die Nacht* depicts a solitary journey not to the Aegean fantasia of Odysseus, nor the Indo-Persian nightlands of Rama and Zarathustra, but to a great and eternal interior space where death gives way to eternal life as naturally as night gives way to day. The journeys into the dark night and the world within are our dynamic and ongoing creations, for, as Novalis observed, "In us, or nowhere, is the Eternal with its worlds, the past and future."[75] This inverted hero's journey was also charted in the same century by Swedenborg, a mechanical genius from Stockholm, who—whether through technique or by divine revelation—recorded highly detailed and self-reflective conversations with angels and devils in a deep meta-reality.

Haglund's violin concerto, also called *Hymnen an die Nacht* (2010), explores the internal landscape in the form of a symphonic poem. Immediately as the concerto opens, and for two and a half minutes as the violin searches, all time and pulse are lost, as it was for Novalis, standing in the night and seeing the dying earth in the distance. Then, the dialogue between violin and orchestra erupts in strife, the chaos of modernity and the orderliness of tradition,

---

74 Georg Philipp Friedrich Freiherr von Hardenberg (1772–1801), pen name Novalis, was a German aristocrat and polymath who was a poet, novelist, philosopher, and mystic.

75 Novalis, *Pollen and Fragments: Selected Poetry and Prose,* trans. Arthur Versluis (Grand Rapids: Phanes Press, 1989), 26.

Novalis, ca. 1799 (Friedrich Freiherr von Hardenberg; 1772-1801), by Friedrich Eduard Eichens (1804–1877), 1845.

an accessory conflict to the greater material-spiritual conflict in Haglund's music. Novalis, Delius, and Swedenborg all saw the same abyss inside themselves, but Delius saw it after Nietzsche and thus, by the poetry of Zarathustra, was seduced inside it. But the violin resists and, like Novalis, presses courageously on into the inner desert at night. Moments of doubt as to the reality of eternity are felt as tremulations against the sublime wall of sound erected by the orchestra. Points of light emerge in the distance, lines and basic platonic forms, and the tips of dawn scatter across the firmament, only to be overwhelmed again by the night, which finally relents in the final minutes with a passage of Dowland-like melodies. Life is restored again, or, as Swedenborg saw it, one has awakened in the next world with new eyes to see. The tension between spirit and flesh has dissolved, and a new, massive swell of gratitude emerges where previously there was only pain and fear of its eternity.

Novalis does not seem to have been influenced by Swedenborg, although the latter died just thirty-four days before the former was born, and yet their lives and ideas intersect with Haglund's work in important ways. From 1716 to 1747, Swedenborg served as an assessor on the Swedish Board of Mines (*Bergskollegium*). Novalis, from 1799 until his death, also served as assessor of mines in Saxony. But whereas Swedenborg describes hell as endless underground cellular chambers flecked with infernal knowledge and insatiable thirst, Novalis saw things just the opposite. There were, in the world below the surface of the earth, "the precious growths that blossom for him in these frightful depths."[76] For many of the German romantic writers of the eighteenth and nineteenth centuries, the journey underground was the discovery of history and the self. Though no one else saw the mine as a metaphor for the soul as clearly as Novalis did, others imagined the depths of the earth as a womb, a crucible for organic and inorganic matter, and something like an inverted Tower of Babel. In Novalis' novel *Heinrich von Ofterdingen*, the anchorite says to his friend the miner, "You [miners] are inverted astronomers . . . For them the sky is

76 Novalis, *Heinrich von Ofterdingen*, trans. Palmer Hilty (Long Grove, IL: Waveland Press, 1990), 71.

the book of the future, while for you the earth reveals monuments of the primal world."[77]

In one of our conversations Tommie said, "Sometimes I have a fear of going under the earth. Particularly when I'm at home, in this house. When I go down to the basement—particularly at nighttime—I don't know what it is, I feel there's something down there that I need to take control over. Maybe I'm just oversensitive. And I have had dreams of going under the earth, a very strong dream. That was in the hospital. I dreamed I was under the earth and there were lots of stones and lions sitting near me. Not doing anything, just sitting next to me, or walking around me. They didn't attack, but they were there. I wanted them to protect me. Something was tempting me to be there. It was a cave. The stones were shining; they were crystalline. They were different colors."

Even if the solitary journey of *Hymnen an die Nacht* is expressly terrestrial, the journey into the earth and the journey into the soul are somehow connected. Though the great journey inward may appear at first dark and lonely, Novalis wrote, "How utterly different will it appear when this darkening is past and the shadow-body is transcended."[78] Haglund's *Hymnen an die Nacht* both charts the inner landscape and forecasts the possibility of the shadowing body's emergence from darkness into light. And, like Beethoven, it revolts against mortal pain by naming it at the hot center, not from a cool and distant orbit, but through perseverance without sentimentality. The thematic foundation of the repertoire is here

77 Novalis, *Heinrich von Ofterdingen*, 86.

78 Novalis, *Pollen and Fragments*, 26.

exposed to its clearest vista. Like Novalis, whose works ranged from spiritual to aesthetic and even political, Haglund draws on a great deal more of tradition than it would seem from the thematic resourcefulness evident in works such as the violin concerto. It is important to see this work as both the key to Haglund's repertoire and also an outlier in that it is the only piece so far with an explicit narrative structure, even if this structure was something of an afterthought.

TWILIGHT

Tommie Haglund sits, reflecting distantly as he speaks, surrounded in a second-floor room by books—including a great number of biographies—in Swedish, English, and a few in German. A framed promotional photo of Laurel and Hardy and an illustration of Donald Duck look over us. Tommie's wife, Elisabet Löfberg Haglund, is here with us some of the time. It is the end of the day, and a thick yellow light is sifting through the room. We have finished listening to a recording of the premiere of the cello concerto, a work that, like the Scandinavian midsummer twilight outside, never quite ends but never feels incomplete. Haglund seems moved by his own work, not tired of it or pressed by my presence to seem untouched. I have asked him to comment on the tensions arising in his work.

ARAM: The cello concerto is an expression of wandering during a painful time. What inspired it?

TOMMIE: It was a time of uncertainty and desperation. What's going to happen with my life? A few years earlier, I'd gone through a traumatic back operation, leaving deep wounds both physical and spiritual—a mixture of sadness, worry, and astonishment mixed with moments of reconciliation with destiny. I think you can hear the despair in the music and that I'm constantly on the border of panic. My heartbeats become drum sequences. Then suddenly, switching over to moments of almost religious gratitude. At that time I was thinking about being united with the cosmos; an urge for that, however that can be translated into sounds.

ARAM: Why did you choose the cello to express pain?

TOMMIE: I didn't choose the cello. I had a commission from Rikskonserter,[79] through my friend John Ehde, the cellist.

ARAM: This concerto feels more inward-looking, like it's the process of you turning yourself inside out, creating a hologram for an inner narrative. And even though you use sounds recorded by NASA in outer space, the feel is that of a journey deep inside the self.

TOMMIE: That's right. The contradictory thing with this concerto is that people have seen it as a description of outer space, but I see the outer space as reflecting inner space in a correspondential way. It's not at all a travelogue of outer space, looking at planets and galaxies, but rather, as you say, an inner journey. People can listen to it how they want, of course.

ARAM: But if someone says they—to speak psychologically—empathize with you through the music, they would need to see it as an introspection rather than a trip on a spaceship. You can go

---

79 Previously, the Swedish Performing Arts Agency (1968-2010), to which symphony orchestras turned for funding for commissions. They also owned the record company, Caprice.

many places from there. But it's most essential to be able to feel what you're feeling.

TOMMIE: It's impossible, I think, to know exactly what someone else is feeling. What is interesting instead is what the music invokes in the listener. You sometimes get people coming to you with these very deep thoughts about your music. All you're trying to do is express your inner life, and when you hear these comments, which take things further than you intended, you feel humbled. There was this conductor from Berlin who wrote to me. He has died now, far too early. But he said the music sounded to him like the night before he was born. That's a very strange thought, but it's fantastic what music can awaken within you.

ARAM: How would you sum up the better part of your musical work?

TOMMIE: Tomas Tranströmer[80] wrote in a poem that everyone has a cathedral inside himself, and in you opens vault after vault, endlessly. You shall never be complete.

80 Swedish poet. He won the Nobel Prize in Literature in 2011.

Afterword

Afterwords are like eulogies. And since this book is the record of a man and his work—a man and a body of work which mean a great deal to me—I feel as if I'm writing a eulogy for a man who still lives and a work that still grows. To take yourself apart and put yourself back together as music—the work of self-realization—takes courage. To make one's inner world directly accessible takes discipline. To trim this experience of its leering excess and numbing ambiguity, to produce a real-time art that possesses the inner world—that's genius. All that really matters is the experience you'll have, if you've yet to have, sitting in the concert hall during *Flaminis Aura* or *La Rosa Profunda*. It almost feels like a séance. I've witnessed members of the audience weeping during the performance, and afterward they get in line to express themselves to the composer, who always receives them graciously.

I've spent hours and hours talking with Tommie and his wife, Elisabet. However it comes across in this text, the format was never a formal sit-down interview. Most of the time, we were in the television room, eating Ricardo's Italian water ice or watching *Fawlty Towers* as we talked. Once, because we were deep in conversation,

Tommie forgot he was roasting a pan full of Szechuan peppers and set off the smoke detectors. Once, I fell asleep while he was explaining something important. We sometimes went into Halmstad to talk and walk around, but Tommie is so recognizable there that we were constantly interrupted. So, we decided to flee to Kalmar, but even there, some people recognized him on the street. I've talked extensively with a lot of composers and artists, and the ones I like most are those who have no upper limit to what they're willing to put themselves through for the work. Talking with Tommie, I always think of Balzac, when he wrote, "If the artist does not throw himself into his work like . . . a miner buried under a fallen roof . . . then the work remains unfinished, it perishes."[81] That's exactly how I see him. And, by the way, there's the underground imagery again, linking Tommie's dreams of caves with Novalis' mine metaphors and Swedenborg's descriptions of the world we build inside us. As Tommie related to me recently about his recent symphony, there are certain passages he himself doesn't quite understand, like hieroglyphics without a Rosetta Stone. This is worth reflecting upon: with what in himself is an artist in touch when he creates something he doesn't himself quite understand?

I should stop making things so complicated, but you see, this is a eulogy for a living man. Eulogies that flatter fall short of reality, and Tommie would be the first to admit he doesn't know where it all will lead. Fittingly, thankfully, the doors keep opening, and there is no end in sight.

---

81 Honoré de Balzac, *Cousin Bette*, trans. Marion Ayton Crawford (New York: Penguin Books, 1965), 215–16.

Appendix: List of complete works by Tommie Haglund

1970 Allegro, for piccolo trumpet and organ, Y1

1972 Largo, for oboe, strings, and harpsichord, Y2

1973 Largo in B Minor, for two violins, guitar, cello, and organ, Y3

ca. 1976 Aforismer (Aphorisms), for guitar, Y4

ca. 1978 Fragment ur en dröm (Fragments of a Dream), for guitar, Y5 [Lost]

ca. 1979 Incidental Music for Brecht's *The Good Person of Szechwan*, for voice and piano, Y5.5 [Lost]

ca. 1980 Incidental Music for *A Midsummer Night's Dream*, for Renaissance consort, Y6

ca. 1981 Incidental Music for Strindberg's *Ghost Sonata*, for solo guitar, Y7

1981 Andante Grazioso, Y8

1987 Notturno (Nocturne), for flute and guitar quintet, Y9

1988 Intensio Animi (Intensity of the Soul), for cello and piano, Y10

1989 Fiori (Flowers), for cello and organ, Y11

1990 Meditation, for piano, Y12a

1990 Meditation, for piano and melody instrument, Y12b

1990 Meditation, for organ, Y12c

1990 Voces (Voices), for chamber orchestra, Y13a

1990 Voces (Voices), for wind quintet and string quintet, Y13b

1990 L'Infinito (Infinity), for violin, Y14

1992 Elif, for string orchestra, Y15

1992 Miraggio (Mirage), for coloratura, soprano, and piano trio, Y16

1994 Min själ (My Soul), for mixed choir, Y17

1995 Inim Inim, for violin and piano, Y18

1996 Fragile, for flute and percussion, Y19a

1996 Fragile, for clavasino, Y19b

1996 Spirarae Celourum (Breathing of Heaven), for clavisino, Y20

1996 Kärlekshjärtan (Love Hearts), double round, for children's choir, string orchestra, piano, and percussion, Y21

1997 To the Sunset Breeze, for guitar, harp, and string quartet, Y22

1998 Arcana Lacrimae (Secret of Tears), for piano, Y23

2000 Morgongåva (Morning gift) (excerpts from Song of Solomon), for tenor and piano, Y24

2001 Flaminis Aura (Cello Concerto), for cello and orchestra, Y25

2001 Il Regno degli Spiriti (Land of Souls), for string quartet, Y26

2001 Varsamt, Victoria sover (Gently, Victoria Is Sleeping), for flute and percussion, Y27

2002 Acedia, for cello and double bass, Y28

2002 Insomnia, for flute, Y29

2003 Röstens dotter (Daughter of the Voice), for violin, clarinet, cello, piano, percussion, and two sopranos, Y30

2004 Stillhet (Stillness), for soprano and cello, Y31

2004 Bortom avsked (Beyond Farewell), for guitar, Y32

2005 Hymnen an die Nacht (Hymns to the night) (Violin Concerto), for violin and orchestra, Y33

2006 Voices of Light, for piano, violin, cello, percussion, flute, and guitar, Y34

2007 Song Cycle: Lamentation, The Dream, La Rosa Profunda, for soprano and piano, Y35

2008 Frammenti (Fragments), for violin, clarinet, and piano, Y36

2009 Cielo Notturno (Night Sky), for cello, Y37

2011 Själens Helgedom (The Sanctuary of the Soul), for mixed choir, Y38a

2013 Sollievo dopo la tempesta (Solace After the Storm), for string trio, Y39

2014	Epilogue to Hymnen an die Nacht, for violin, Y40
2014	Serenata per Diotima (Serenade for Diotima), for string orchestra, Y41
2015	Själens Helgedom (The Sanctuary of the Soul), for brass ensemble, Y38b
2015	Di Sogni Tessuto (Woven in Dreams), for organ, Y42
2016	La Rosa Profunda, for soprano and orchestra, Y43
2016	Rosa Profunda Alborada, for violin and piano, Y44
2020	Symphony, for orchestra, Y45
2021	Making Something out of Nothing (male voice), Y46a
2021	Making Something out of Nothing (female voice), Y46b

Note: This definitive opus numbering system for Tommie Haglund's musical output was developed as a part of the research for this book. In keeping with tradition in musicological research, the first letter of the researcher's surname has been used as a prefix for the numbers.

Bibliography

Bach, Richard. *Illusions: The Adventures of a Reluctant Messiah*. New York: Delta Trade Paperbacks, 1998.

Balzac, Honoré de. *Cousin Bette*. Translated by Marion Ayton Crawford. New York: Penguin Books, 1965.

Barnard, Nick. "Recording of the Month: Flaminis Aura: Works by Tommie Haglund." *MusicWeb International*, July 2017. https://www.musicweb-international.com/classrev/2017/Jul/Haglund_flaminis_BIS2025.htm.

Bergquist, Lars, ed. *Swedenborg's Dream Diary*. Translated by Anders Hallengren. Royersford: Swedenborg Foundation, 2024.

Björkman, Stig, Torsten Manns, and Jonas Sima. *Bergman on Bergman*. Translated by Paul Britten Austin. New York: Simon and Schuster, 1973.

Calvocoressi, Richard and Katharina Schulz. *Oskar Kokoschka, 1886–1980*. New York: S.R. Guggenheim Museum, 1987.

Carley, Lionel. *Frederick Delius: Music, Art and Literature*. Aldershot, UK: Ashgate Publishing Limited, 1998.

Cleese, John. *So: The Autobiography*. London: Random House, 2014.

Colles, Henry Cope [writing anonymously]. "The Delius Festival: A Retrospect." *The Times*, November 2, 1929.

Cowley, Malcolm. "Introduction." In *Writers at Work: The Paris Review Interviews*, vol. 1, edited by Malcolm Cowley, 3-21. New York: Viking, 1958.

Deutsch, Otto Erich. *Mozart: A Documentary Biography*. London: Adam & Charles Black, 1965.

Fenby, Eric. *Delius As I Knew Him*. Mineola, NY: Dover, 1994 [1936].

Gritten, Anthony. "Delius, Whoever He May Be." *The Delius Society Journal*, no. 160 (2016): 61–73.

Hallengren, Anders. *Grand Theme and Other Essays*. London: Swedenborg Society, 2013.

Hölderlin, Friedrich. *Poems of Friedrich Hölderlin: The Fire of the Gods Drives Us to Set Forth by Day and by Night*. Translated by James Mitchell. San Francisco: Ithuriel's Spear, 2007.

Holmqvist, Åke. *Beethoven biografin*. Stockholm: Bonnier, 2012.

Jenkins, Lyndon and Paul Guinery. *Delius & Fenby: A Photographic Journey*. Walsall, UK: The Delius Society of Great Britain, 2004.

Jung, Carl. *The Red Book*. New York: W.W. Norton, 2012.

Lamm, Martin. *Emanuel Swedenborg: The Development of His Thought*. Translated by Tomas Spiers and Anders Hallengren. West Chester, PA: Swedenborg Foundation, 2000.

Lee-Browne, Martin & Paul Guinery. *Delius and His Music*. Woodbridge, UK: Boydell Press, 2014.

Levy, Julien. *Arshile Gorky*. New York: Harry N. Abrams, 1966.

Ley, Stephen, ed. *Beethovens Leben in authentischen Bildern und Texten*. Berlin: B. Cassirer, 1925.

Munch, Edvard. *The Private Journals of Edvard Munch: We Are Flames Which Pour Out of the Earth*. Edited and translated by J. Gill Holland. Madison: University of Wisconsin Press, 2004.

Novalis. *Hymns to the Night and Other Selected Writings*. Translated by Charles E. Passage. New York: Liberal Arts Press, 1960.

Novalis. *Pollen and Fragments: Selected Poetry and Prose.* Translated by Arthur Versluis. Grand Rapids: Phanes Press, 1989.

Novalis. *Heinrich von Ofterdingen.* Translated by Palmer Hilty. Long Grove, IL: Waveland Press, 1990.

Olsson, Olle, ed. *Electronic Music in Sweden.* Stockholm: The Swedish Music Information Center, 1985.

Origen. *Homilies on Leviticus: 1–16.* Translated by Gary Wayne Barkley. Washington, DC: Catholic University of America Press, 1990.

Oyler, Philip T. "Delius at Grèz." *The Musical Times* 113, no. 1551 (1972): 444–447.

Oyler, Philip T. *The Generous Earth.* London: Pallas Athene, 2002 (1950).

Pålsson, Hans. *Tankar om musik.* Stockholm: Prisma, 2002.

Poulton, Diana. *John Dowland.* Berkeley: University of California Press, 1982.

Prideaux, Sue. *Edvard Munch: Behind the Scream.* New Haven: Yale University Press, 2005.

Quist, Robert. *The History of Modern Swedish Music.* Lewiston, NY: The Edwin Mellen Press, 2010.

Rubin, Bruce Joel. *Jacob's Ladder.* New York: Applause Theatre Book Publishers, 1989.

Rushton, Julian. *Mozart: His Life and Work.* Oxford: Oxford University Press, 2006.

Swedenborg, Emanuel. *Swedenborgs Drömbok: glädjen och det stora kvalet.* Translated by Lars Bergquist. Stockholm: Norstedt, 1988. [Author's translation used in epigraph.]

Swedenborg, Emanuel. *Heaven and Hell.* Translated by George F. Dole. West Chester, PA: Swedenborg Foundation, 2000.

Swedenborg, Emanuel. *On Tremulation.* Translated by CT Odhner. Bryn Athyn, PA: Swedenborg Scientific Association, 2005.

Swedenborg, Emanuel. *Divine Love and Wisdom.* Translated by George F. Dole. West Chester, PA: Swedenborg Foundation, 2010.

Swedenborg, Emanuel. *The Worship and Love of God.* Translated by Alfred H. Stroh and Frank Sewall. West Chester, PA: Swedenborg Foundation, 2020.

Taylor, Michael R., ed. *Arshile Gorky: A Retrospective.* Philadelphia: Philadelphia Museum of Art, 2010.

Wallrup, Erik. *Being Musically Attuned: The Act of Listening to Music.* Farnham, UK: Ashgate Publishing Limited, 2015.

Wood, Robin. *Ingmar Bergman.* New ed. Edited by Barry Keith Grant. Detroit: Wayne State University Press, 2013.

Further Listening

Alfvén, Hugo. *Midsommarvaka* / Swedish Rhapsody No. 1 / Symphony no. 2 in D Major. Compact disc. Djursholm, Sweden: BIS, 1988.

Bach, Johann Sebastian. Brandenburg Concertos. Academy of Ancient Music, Richard Egarr. Compact disc. Arles, France: Harmonia Mundi, 2009.

Beethoven, Ludwig van. Symphonies Nos. 1–9. Konstantin Scherbakov, piano. Compact disc. Hong Kong: Naxos, 2006.

Delius, Frederick. *Song of the High Hills*. Royal Philharmonic Orchestra, Eric Fenby. Compact disc. London: Unicorn-Kanchana, 1984.

Delius, Frederick. *Florida Suite / North Country Sketches*. Compact disc. London: Chandos, 1986.

Delius, Frederick. Double Concerto / Violin Concerto / Cello Concerto. BBC Symphony Orchestra, Hallé Orchestra, Sir Andrew Davis. Compact disc. Colchester, UK: Chandos, 2011.

Delius, Frederick. *The Walk to the Paradise Garden / A Song of Summer* / etc. London Symphony Orchestra, Sir John Barbirolli. Compact disc. London: EMI Classics, 2011.

Dowland, John. *Seven Teares: Music of John Dowland*. Compact disc. Arles, France: Harmonia Mundi, 2002.

Hába, Alois. Violin Works / etc. Compact disc. Prague: Subraphon, 1997.

Haglund, Tommie. *Inim-Inim*. Compact disc. Stockholm: Caprice, 1997.

Haglund, Tommie, et al. *Kingám: New Swedish Flute Music*. Compact disc. Huddinge, Sweden: Nosag, 2003.

Haglund, Tommie. *Hymns to the Night*. Compact disc. Stockholm: Phono Suecia, 2010.

Haglund, Tommie. *Flaminis Aura*. Compact disc. Åkersberga, Sweden: BIS, 2017.

Janáček, Leoš. String Quartet No. 1 / String Quartet No. 2 "Intimate Letters." Juilliard String Quartet. Compact disc. New York: Sony Classical, 1996.

Johanson, Sven-Eric. *Sven-Eric Johanson*. Compact disc. Stockholm: Proprius, 1995.

Johanson, Sven-Eric. *Rotas Tenet*. Compact disc. Styrsö, Sweden: Slask, 1994.

Maderna, Bruno. *Maderna*. Vol. 17. Compact disc. Milan: Arkadia, 1992.

Melchiorre, Alessandro. *Terra Incognita*. Compact disc. Milan: Edizioni Casa Ricordi, 1999.

Mellnäs, Arne. *Nocturnes / Rendez-vous 1 / L'Infinito / Transparence*. Compact disc. Stockholm: Phono Suecia, 1988.

Mozart, Wolfgang Amadeus. *Klavierkonzerte*. Wiener Symphoniker, Rudolf Buchbinder. Compact disc. Neuhausen, Germany: Profil Medien, 2004.

Rameau, Jean-Philippe. *Acante et Céphise / Les fêtes d'Hébé*. Compact disc. San Lorenzo del Escorial, Spain: Glossa, 1998.

Scelsi, Giacinto. *The Orchestral Works 1*. Compact disc. New York: Mode, 2001.

Scelsi, Giacinto. *The Orchestral Works 2*. Compact disc. New York: Mode, 2006.

Schubert, Franz. Symphony No. 4 in C Minor, D. 417 *Tragic*. Academy of St. Martin-in-the-Fields, Neville Marriner. Compact disc. Holland: Philips, 1987.

Thompson, Dr. Jeffrey and Richard Stamper. *Song of Earth: NASA Space Recordings of Earth*. Compact disc. Carlsbad, CA: Brain/Mind Research, 1991.

Various. *Esprit D'Arménie*. Jordi Savall, rebeckha, viola. Compact disc. Bellaterra, Spain: Alia Vox, 2012.

Victoria, Tomás Luis de. *Music of Tomás Luis de Victoria*. Compact disc. Troy, NY: Dorian Discovery, 1996.

Source: Department of Swedenborgiana and New Church Collections, Swedenborg Library, Bryn Athyn, PA

Engraving of Emanuel Swedenborg at the age of 80 by W. Holl from original picture in the Exegetic Society in Stockholm. Based on a lithograph done by J. F. Martin in 1782.

About Emanuel Swedenborg

EMANUEL SWEDENBORG (1688–1772) was born Emanuel Swedberg (or Svedberg) in Stockholm, Sweden, on January 29, 1688. He was the third of the nine children of Jesper Swedberg (1653–1735) and Sara Behm (1666–1696). His father, a Lutheran clergyman, later became a celebrated and controversial bishop.

After studying at the University of Uppsala (1699–1709), Emanuel journeyed to England, Holland, France, and Germany to study and work with leading scientists in Western Europe. Upon his return, he apprenticed as an engineer under the brilliant Swedish inventor Christopher Polhem (1661–1751). Emanuel gained favor with Sweden's King Charles XII, who gave him a salaried position as an overseer of Sweden's mining industry. Although he was engaged, he never married.

After the death of Charles XII, Emanuel was ennobled by Queen Ulrika Eleonora, and his last name was changed to Swedenborg (or Svedenborg). This change in status gave him a seat in the Swedish House of Nobles, where he remained an active participant in the Swedish government throughout his life.

As a member of the Royal Swedish Academy of Sciences, Swedenborg devoted himself to scientific studies and philosophical reflections that culminated in a number of publications. It was during the later part of his life and career, from age 55 to his death in 1772 at the age of 84, that he experienced continuous conscious interaction with the other world. Following on from his training in observation as a scientist, Swedenborg meticulously detailed his experiences in neo-Latin and devoted his life to publishing his transformed perspective on spirituality, philosophy, and Christianity.

Today's readers benefit from both the published and posthumously published works of Swedenborg, which have continued to be made available by publishers, archivists, librarians, and translators in the centuries since his death. *Heaven and Hell* is his most popular work, and it is in his multi-volume series *Arcana Coelestia* (*Secrets of Heaven*) that he presents a non-literal reading of the bible, using what he calls "correspondences."

You can learn more about Swedenborg's life and work at swedenborg.com.

About the Swedenborg Foundation

THIS BOOK WAS produced by the Swedenborg Foundation, an independent nonprofit organization dedicated to making Emanuel Swedenborg's thought more widely known and freely available to all. The Swedenborg Foundation is a nonprofit organization supported by the contributions of individuals and foundations. All the books we publish are made possible by the generous support of our donors.

Connect with us at www.swedenborg.com to support this and other publishing projects, learn about membership opportunities, and purchase or freely access Swedenborg's writings.